Nicky Epstein
Enchanted Knits for Dolls

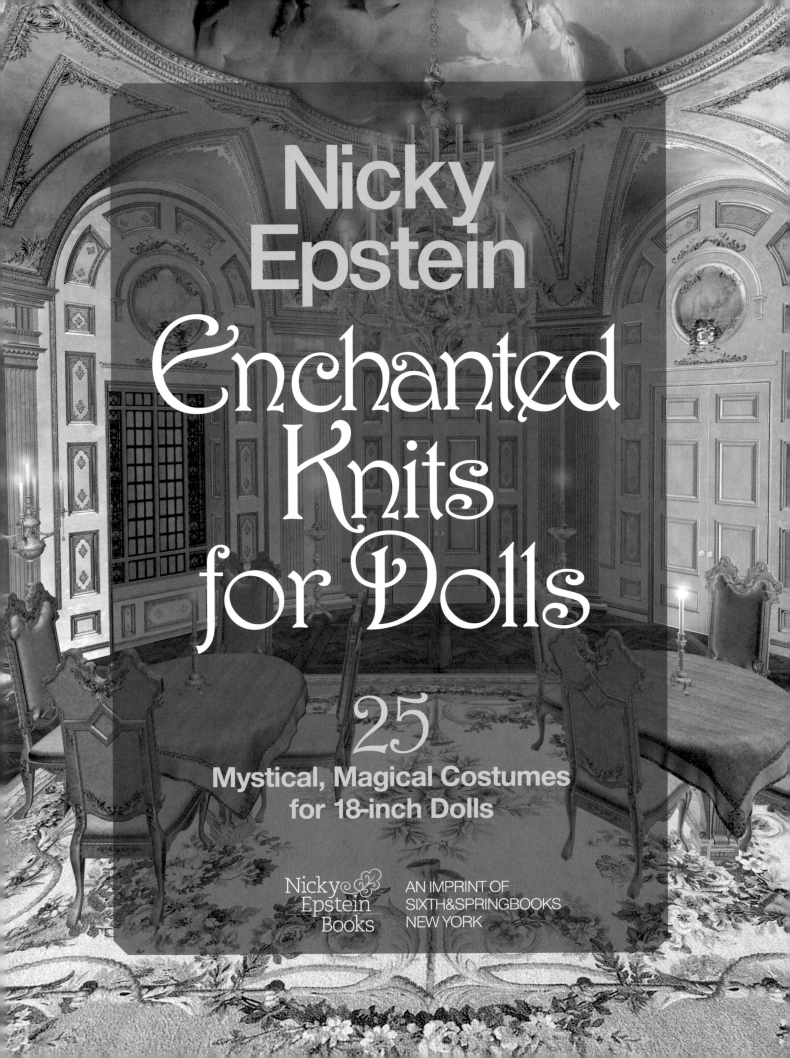

Nicky Epstein
Enchanted Knits for Dolls

25
Mystical, Magical Costumes for 18-inch Dolls

Nicky
Epstein
Books

AN IMPRINT OF
SIXTH&SPRINGBOOKS
NEW YORK

Nicky Epstein Books

AN IMPRINT OF SIXTH&SPRING BOOKS
161 AVENUE OF THE AMERICAS, NEW YORK NY 10013
SIXTHANDSPRINGBOOKS.COM

Managing Editor
LAURA COOKE

Senior Editor
LISA SILVERMAN

Yarn Editor
VANESSA PUTT

Supervising
Patterns Editor
CARLA SCOTT

Patterns Editors
LISA BUCCELLATO
LORI STEINBERG

Technical Illustrations
LORETTA DACHMAN
LORI STEINBERG

Photography
JACK DEUTSCH

Stylist
KATHY NORTH

Vice President
TRISHA MALCOLM

Creative Director
JOE VIOR

Publisher
CAROLINE KILMER

Production Manager
DAVID JOINNIDES

President
ART JOINNIDES

Chairman
JAY STEIN

Library of Congress
Cataloging-in-Publication Data
Epstein, Nicky.
Enchanted Knits for Dolls : 25 mystical,
magical costumes for 18-inch dolls / Nicky
Epstein. — First [edition].
    pages cm
ISBN 978-1-936096-92-3
1. Doll clothes—Patterns.
2. Knitting—Patterns. I. Title.
TT175.7.E76 2015
746.43'2043—dc23
                        2015006832

Manufactured in China

1 3 5 7 9 10 8 6 4 2

First Edition

To all the children, like Sofia,
Mason, Marian, John, Jada, and Anthony, who believe...
and to children of all ages who still believe and
stay forever enchanted.

Contents

12 Snow Queen   **16** Pirate Queen

36 Kids' Hood   **38** Fairy Godmother

60 Wonderful Wizard   **64** Golden Princess

88 Guardian Angel   **92** Monster Mash   **96** Kids' Hat & Wristlets

Once Upon a Time...

These words have taken us to magical castles, mythical woods, adventurous roads, and lands of enchantment. We have encountered wizards, witches, princesses, and mermaids. We have walked with Red Riding Hood, run with Cinderella, and flown with Peter Pan. And now their garments can be knitted!

This magical book is for the young and the young at heart (I am with the latter group) . . . a book of knits for dolls using enchanted storybook images and characters. We knew them as children, have carried them with us into adulthood, and love passing them on to future generations.

The designs in the book are geared toward different skill levels: some are time-consuming and some can be quick gifts. But I particularly want to encourage you to open the world of knitting to children. The how-to-knit ponchos and purse on pages 112–115 are the perfect beginner projects to teach children to knit and inspire them to create their own magical knitted pieces—a skill for which they will thank you for the rest of their lives.

So share my 29th book with children, and have fun making and playing with these special garments for your special princes and princesses and their favorite dolls. Grab your needles and yarn and come with me into the woods, under the sea, up in the air . . . and enjoy these enchanted knits.

NICKY EPSTEIN

NOTE: The sizes of different dolls may vary slightly. I encourage you to take the measurements of your own doll and compare them with those given in the instructions, to ensure a good fit.

The Projects

Snow Queen

●●●○

*"The Snow Queen Loves the Cold and Ice
She Makes a Winter Paradise"*

MATERIALS
- 2 1¾oz/50g skeins (each approx 126yd/115m) of Bergère de France *Sonora* (cotton/acrylic) each in #21985 eclat (A) and #21996 vapeur (B) (4)
- 1 1¾oz/50g skein (each approx 87yd/80m) of Bergère de France *Teddy* (polyamide) each in #20980 blanche-neige (C) and #29377 ciel (D) (4)
- 1 1¾oz/50g skein (each approx 87yd/80m) of Bergère de France *Metalika* (polyamide/metal-effect poly-ester) in #21756 libellule (E)
- One pair size 7 (4.5mm) needles OR SIZE TO OBTAIN GAUGE
- 5 snaps
- 1 rhinestone snowflake button (La Mode #2008)
- 2 packages Jolee's Boutique Dimensional Stickers, #50-20428 Snowflake repeats
- Small amount of white tissue paper for sticker backing
- Yarn needle for duplicate stitch
- ½yd/.5m of ¼"/.5cm blue satin ribbon
- Sewing needle
- Sewing thread
- Stitch markers
- Stitch holders
- Piece of silver faux leather, approx 12"/30.5cm long and 2"/5cm high, for belt

GAUGE
17 sts and 23 rows to 4"/10cm over simple seed st using size 7 (4.5mm) needles and 1 strand each of A and E held tog.
TAKE TIME TO CHECK GAUGE.

SIMPLE SEED STITCH
(multiple of 4 sts, plus 2)
Row 1 (RS) K1, *k3, p1; rep from *, end k1.
Row 2 and all WS rows Purl.
Rows 3 and 7 Knit.
Row 5 K2, *p1, k3; rep from * to end.
Row 8 Purl.
Rep rows 1–8 for simple seed st.

GOWN
FRONT
With C, cast on 50 sts. Knit 6 rows.
Cut C.
With 1 strand each of A and E held tog, knit 1 row, purl 1 row.
Work in simple seed st until piece measures 7½"/19cm from beg, end with a WS row.

SHAPE WAIST
Next row (RS) K1, [k2tog] 24 times, k1—26 sts.
Work 3 rows in St st, then beg with row 1 and work in simple seed st for 1½"/4cm more.

SHAPE ARMHOLES
Bind off 2 sts at beg of next 2 rows, then 1 st at beg of next 2 rows—20 sts.
Cont in pat as established until armhole measures 1½"/4cm.
Bind off.

BACK
Work same as front until waist shaping is complete —26 sts.
Purl 1 row on WS.

DIVIDE FOR BACK OPENING
RIGHT BACK
Next row (RS) K13 for right back, cast on 4 sts for placket, turn. Place rem 13 sts on a st holder for left back, and cont on 17 sts for right back as foll:
Next row (WS) [P1, k1] twice for back band, p13, [p1, k1] twice for back band.
Next row (RS) K1, *k3, p1; rep from * to last 4 sts, [p1, k1] twice.
Cont working 4 sts at center edge in k1, p1 rib and rem 13 sts in simple seed st as established, until right back measures same as front to armhole, end with a WS row.

SHAPE ARMHOLE
Next row (RS) Bind off 2 sts, work to end—15 sts.
Next row Work even in pats.
Next row (RS) Bind off 1 st, work to end—14 sts.
Next row Work even in pats.
Cont in pats until armhole measures 1½"/4cm. Bind off.

LEFT BACK
Next row (RS) With RS facing, join A and E, cast on 4 sts for placket, [k1, p1] twice over these sts, knit to end.
Next row (WS) P13, [k1, p1] twice.
Next row (RS) [K1, p1] twice, *k3, p1; rep from *, end k1.
Cont 4 sts at center edge in k1, p1 rib and rem 13 sts in simple seed st as established, until left back measures same as front to armhole, end with a RS row.
Next row (WS) Bind off 2 sts, work to end—15 sts.
Next row Work even in pats.
Next row (RS) Bind off 1 st, work to end—14 sts.
Next row Work even in pats.
Cont in pat as established until armhole measures 1½"/4cm. Bind off.

SLEEVES
With C, cast on 20 sts. Knit 6 rows. Cut C.
Next (inc) row (RS) With 1 strand each of A and E held tog, CO1, knit to end, CO1—22 sts.
Purl 1 row.

Work in simple seed st pattern for 6 more rows.
Next row (RS) CO1, work in pat to end, CO1—24 sts.
Work inc'd sts into pat, cont until sleeve measures 3"/7.5cm from beg, end with a WS row.

SHAPE CAP
Bind off 2 sts at beg of next 2 rows, 1 st at beg of next 2 rows—18 sts.
Work 4 rows even in pat as established.
Dec row (RS) Ssk, work to last 2 sts, k2tog—16 sts.
Dec row (WS) P2tog, work to last 3 sts, p2tog tbl—14 sts.
Rep last 2 rows twice more—6 sts rem.
Next row (RS) Ssk, bind off to last 2 sts, k2tog. Fasten off last st.

FINISHING
Sew shoulder seams.

NECKBAND
With RS facing and C, pick up and k 40 sts evenly around neck. Knit 1 row. Bind off. Sew side seams. Sew sleeve seams. Set in sleeves.
Sew snaps evenly along back opening. Sew snowflake button to front of dress, just below collar. Sew snowflake stickers to gown as desired.
Note that snowflakes are also used for earrings. Tissue paper is used on the backs of the ribbon stickers to prevent sticking to objects.

CAPE
With D, cast on 86 sts.
Knit 6 rows for border. Cut D.
With 1 strand each of B and E held tog, work 6 rows in St st.
Dec row (RS) K2tog, knit to last 2 sts, ssk—84 sts.
Next row Purl.
Cont in St st and rep dec row every 6th row 13 more times—58 sts. Work even until cape measures 14"/35.5cm from beg, end with a WS row.
Dec row (RS) [K1, k2tog] 19 times, k1—39 sts.
Purl 1 row. Cut B and E.

COLLAR
Next row (RS) With D, CO1, knit to end, CO1—41 sts.
Next row Purl.
Rep last 2 rows 4 more times—49 sts. Bind off.

FRONT EDGING
With RS facing and D, pick up and k 79 sts evenly along right front edge, between the border and collar.
Next row (WS) Knit.
Bind off knitwise.
Repeat along left front edge.
Work cast-on and bind-off tails of edging into the collar and border.

FINISHING
Cut ribbon in two equal lengths, and sew one to each side of front edging, just below collar.
Sew snowflake stickers to cape as desired, and to ribbons.

HAT
With D, cast on 56 sts. Work in St st for 3"/7.5cm, end with a RS row.
Dec row (WS) Purl across, dec 4 sts evenly spaced—52 sts. Cut D.

SHAPE CROWN
With 1 strand each of B and E held tog, knit 1 row, purl 1 row.
Row 1 (RS) K1, [SK2P, k7] 5 times, k1—42 sts.
Row 2 and all WS rows Purl.
Row 3 K1, [SK2P, k5] 5 times, k1—32 sts.
Row 5 K1, [SK2P, k3] 5 times, k1—22 sts.
Row 7 K1, [SK2P, k1] 5 times, k1—12 sts.
Cut yarn, leaving a long tail. Thread tail through rem 12 sts. Pull tightly to gather, and secure. Sew side edges tog. Sew snowflake stickers to hat as desired.

BELT
Cut faux leather to fit around doll's waist, with a slight overlap for snap. Using photo as guide, trim leather to a point in the middle and decorate with stickers. Sew snap to ends. ✷

Pirate Queen

*"A Pirate Sails the Oceans Blue
And Plunders with Her Merry Crew"*

MATERIALS
- 1 1¾oz/50g skein (each approx 202yd/185m) of Lion Brand *Vanna's Glamour* (acrylic/metallic polyester) each in #100 diamond (A), #151 grey stone (B), #114 red stone (C), and #171 gold (D) (2)
- Rainbow Yarns elastic thread in white and gray (or any black elastic thread) to gather flared sleeves and cuffs
- 13"/33cm of ¼" black elastic for eye patch
- Small piece of black felt for eye patch
- Purchased skull and crossbones for bag
- One pair size 3 (3.25mm) needles OR SIZE TO OBTAIN GAUGE
- Size D/3 (3.25mm) crochet hook
- Stitch markers
- 3 small stitch holders

GAUGE
24 sts and 36 rows to 4"/10cm over St st (knit on RS, purl on WS) using size 3 (3.25mm) needles.
TAKE TIME TO CHECK GAUGE.

STITCH GLOSSARY
CO1 (cast on 1—increase) Wrap yarn around left thumb from back to front. Insert RH needle from front into the loop on thumb. Remove thumb from loop and tighten loop on needle (also called wrap cast-on). 1 stitch has been increased.

BLOUSE
BACK
With A, cast on 41 sts. Knit 3 rows.
Next row (WS) K3, p to last 3 sts, k3. Cont in St st, keeping first and last 3 sts in garter st (knit every row) as established until piece measures 1½"/4cm from beg, end with a WS row.
Next (inc) row (RS) Kfb, knit to last st, kfb—43 sts.
Cont in St st only until back measures 4"/10cm from beg, end with a WS row.

SHAPE ARMHOLE
Bind off 3 sts at beg of next 2 rows, 2 sts at beg of next 2 rows—33 sts.
Work even until armhole measures 2¾"/7cm, end with a WS row.
Bind off 8 sts, k to last 8 sts and place these 17 sts on st holder, bind off rem 8 sts.

FRONT
Note Front is shorter than back to armhole.

Work same as back until piece measures 1¼"/3cm from beg.
Next (inc) row (RS) Kfb, k to last st, kfb—43 sts.
Cont in St st only until back measures 3¾"/9.5cm from beg, end with a WS row.

SHAPE ARMHOLE
Bind off 3 sts at beg of next 2 rows, 2 sts at beg of next 2 rows—33 sts.

BEG FRONT DETAIL
Row 1 (RS) K11, [p1, k1] 5 times, p1, k11.
Row 2 P11, [k1, p1] 5 times, k1, p11.
Rep rows 1 and 2 twice more.

DIVIDE FOR NECK
Next row (RS) K11, [p1, k1] twice, p1, join 2nd ball of A, bind off 1 st, cont in pats as established to end—16 sts each side of neck.
Working both sides at once with separate balls of yarn, cont as established until armhole measures 2¼"/5.5cm, end with a RS row.

LEFT FRONT
Next row (WS) Rib 5 sts and sl to holder, bind off 3 sts, purl to end.
Work even on rem 8 sts until armhole measures 2¾"/7cm, end with a WS row. Bind off.

RIGHT FRONT
Work 1 row on WS side.
Next row (RS) Rib 5 sts and sl to holder, bind off 3 sts, knit to end.
Work even on rem 8 sts until armhole measures 2¾"/7cm, end with a WS row. Bind off.

SLEEVES (make 2)
With A, cast on 50 sts.
Knit 3 rows. Work in St st until piece

measures 1"/2.5cm from beg, end with a WS row.

Row (dec) 1 (RS) [K2tog] 25 times—25 sts.

Row 2 (WS) *P1, k1; rep from * to last st, p1.

Rows 3–6 K the knit sts and p the purl sts.

Row (inc) 7 (RS) K1, *kfb, k1; rep from * to end—37 sts.

Row 8 Purl one row on WS, inc 3 sts evenly across—40 sts.

Cont in St st until sleeve measures 4"/10cm from beg, end with a WS row.

SHAPE CAP

Bind off 3 sts at beg of next 2 rows, bind off 1 st at beg of next 2 rows—32 sts. Work even until sleeve cap measures 1"/2.5cm, end with a WS row.

Next (dec) row (RS) K2tog, k to last 2 sts, ssk—30 sts.

Next row Purl.

Rep last 2 rows once—28 sts.

Next (dec) row (RS) [K3tog] 9 times, k1—10 sts.

Next (dec) row [P2tog] 5 times—5 sts. Bind off.

FINISHING

Sew shoulder seams.

COLLAR

With RS facing, rib 5 sts from right front holder, pick up and k 12 sts along right neck edge, k17 from back neck holder, pick up and k 12 sts along left neck edge, rib 5 sts from left front holder—51 sts. Work in k1, p1 rib as established until collar measures 2"/5cm. Bind off in rib.

Sew side and sleeve seams. Set sleeves into armholes.

With crochet hook and D, make a chain approx 18"/46cm. Using photo as guide, lace through sts on each side of neck opening, keeping chain even and crossing twice. Knot each end.

Thread elastic through rib at sleeve cuffs.

VEST

Note Vest is worked in one piece.

With C, cast on 54 sts.

Beg with a RS row, work 2 rows in St st.

SHAPE FRONT EDGES

Next (inc) row (RS) CO1, knit to end of row, CO1—56 sts.

Next row Purl.

Rep last 2 rows 4 more times—64 sts. Work even until piece measures 1¾"/4.5cm from beg, end with a WS row.

DIVIDE FOR FRONTS AND BACK

Next row (RS) K 13 sts for right front and sl to holder, bind off 4 sts for right armhole, work until 30 sts are on needle for back and sl to holder, bind off 4 sts for left armhole, knit to end—13 left front sts.

LEFT FRONT

Cont on 13 sts for left front, work in St st until armhole measures 2½"/6.5cm, end with a WS row.

SHAPE NECK

Next (dec) row (RS) Knit to last 2 sts, k2tog—12 sts.

Next row Purl.

Rep last 2 rows 3 more times—9 sts. Work 2 rows even. Bind off rem sts for left front shoulder.

RIGHT FRONT

Slip 13 sts to needle, ready for a WS row. Join C and work in St st until armhole measures 2½"/6.5cm, end with a WS row.

SHAPE NECK

Next (dec) row (RS) Ssk, knit to end—12 sts.

Next row Purl.

Rep last 2 rows 3 more times—9 sts. Work 2 rows even. Bind off rem 9 sts for right front shoulder.

BACK

Slip 30 sts to needle, ready for a WS row. Join C and work in St st until armhole measures 2½"/6.5cm, end with a WS row.

SHAPE SHOULDERS

Bind off 9 sts for left back shoulder, work until there are 12 sts on needle for back neck and sl to holder, bind off rem sts for right back shoulder.

FINISHING

Sew shoulder seams.

ARMHOLE TRIM

With RS facing, crochet hook and C, work 30 sc evenly around armhole edges.

EDGE TRIM

Beg at center back neck, work sl st crochet evenly around outer edge of vest.

PANTALOONS (make 2 pieces)

With B, cast on 52 sts. Knit 3 rows. Beg with a WS row, work in St st until piece measures 1½"/4cm from beg, end with a WS row.

Next (dec) row (RS) *K2, k2tog; rep from * to end—39 sts.

Next row (WS) P1, *k1, p1; rep from * to end.

K the knit sts and p the purl sts for k1, p1 rib for 4 more rows.

SHAPE LEGS

Work in St st, inc 1 st each side every 6th row 3 times—45 sts. Work even until piece measures 4"/10cm from beg.

SHAPE CROTCH

Bind off 4 sts at beg of next 2 rows, 1 st at beg of next 4 rows—33 sts.

Cont in St st for 2¼"/5.5cm more.

Work in k1, p1 rib for 4 rows. Bind off.

FINISHING

Fold each leg in half and sew from cast-on edge to crotch shaping. Sew center front seam from crotch to rib. Rep for center back seam. Thread elastic through rib at cuffs and waistband.

KERCHIEF

With D, cast on 86 sts. Knit 4 rows. Beg with RS row, work 4 rows in St st.

Next (dec) row (RS) K1, ssk, k to last 3 sts, k2tog, k1—84 sts.

Next row Purl.

Rep last 2 rows 40 more times—4 sts.

Next row (RS) Ssk, k2tog—2 sts.

Next row P2tog. Fasten off.

Knot 2 ends of cast-on row tog, measuring to fit around your doll's head.

BOOTY BAG

With D, cast on 15 sts. Knit 4 rows. Work in St st until piece measures 6"/15cm from beg, end with a RS row.

Beg with a WS row, knit 6 rows. Bind off. Place removable marker at 2½"/7.5cm from cast-on edge for fold line.

STRAP

With D, cast on 7 sts.

Next row (RS) [K1, p1] 3 times, k1.

K the knit sts and p the purl sts for k1, p1 rib until strap measures 10"/25.5cm. Bind off.

FINISHING

Fold cast-on edge of bag to RS at marker and sew side seams. Sew strap to sides. Sew skull and crossbones to front of bag.

EYE PATCH

Cut felt into eyeglass shape. Sew elastic to either side to fit doll's forehead. ✳

Rapunzel

●●●○

*"Rapunzel's Hair Is So Lowdown:
Her Hairdresser Is Out of Town"*

MATERIALS
- 1 1¾oz/50g cone (each approx 143yd/131m) of Skacel Collection *Karat* (polyester metallic) in #04 light gold metallic (A) (3)
- 2 cones in #18 purple metallic (B)
- 1 .88oz/25g cone (each approx 108yd/100m) of Skacel Collection *Vegas* (rayon/polyester metallic) in #05 light pink metallic (C) (3)
- 1 3½oz/100g hank (each approx 110yd/101m) of Plymouth Yarn *Baby Alpaca Grande* (baby alpaca) in #1100 sun mist (or color to match your doll's hair) (D) [YARN WT = 5]
- 3–4yd/3–3.5m of any novelty glitter yarn (for hair)
- One pair size 4 (3.5mm) needles OR SIZE TO OBTAIN GAUGE
- Size 4 (3.5mm) circular needle, 24"/60cm long
- Size E/4 (3.5mm) crochet hook
- Small amount of elastic thread for flared cuffs
- 3 snaps
- Sewing needle and thread
- Pointy hat form or manila folder and template (page TK)
- Lavender tulle, 36"/91.5cm wide and 5"/12.5cm high, for hat decoration
- Glue
- Stitch markers
- Stitch holders

GAUGE
24 sts and 32 rows to 4"/10cm over St st (knit on RS, purl on WS) using size 4 (3.5mm) needles and B or C. TAKE TIME TO CHECK GAUGE.

STITCH GLOSSARY
CS (catch strand) Insert RH needle under the loose strand of A and knit the next st on the LH needle, catching the strand behind the new st.
LD (lift and decrease) Insert RH needle under the loose strand of A and knit the next 3 sts on LH needle tog, catching the strand behind the new st.

QUILTING PATTERN
(multiple of 6 sts plus 3)
Row 1 (WS) With A, k1, p1, *sl 5 wyib, p1; rep from * to last st, end k1.
Row 2 With B, knit.
Row 3 With B, k1, purl to last st, k1.

Row 4 With A, k1, sl 3 wyib, *CS, sl 5 wyib; rep from * to last 5 sts, CS, sl 3 wyib, k1.
Row 5 With A, k1, sl 3 wyib, *p1, sl 5 wyib; rep from * to last 5 sts, end p1, sl 3 wyib, k1.
Rows 6 and 7 With B, rep rows 2 and 3.
Row 8 With A, k1, *CS, sl 5 wyib; rep from * to last 2 sts, end CS, k1.
Rep rows 1–8 for quilting pat.

TRACKS PATTERN
(multiple of 10 sts)
Row 1 (WS) *P6, k4; rep from * across.
Row 2 and all RS rows Knit.
Row 3 and 7 Purl.
Row 5 *P1, k4, p5; rep from * across.
Row 8 Rep row 2.
Rep rows 1–8 for tracks pat.

NOTE
1) Skirt is worked in 3 separate pieces from hem to bodice. The sides are worked with A and B in quilting pat and the front (insert) is worked with C in tracks pat. The pieces are seamed at front before the bodice is worked.

LEFT SIDE OF SKIRT
With A, cast on 63 sts. Knit 1 row on RS. Rep rows 1–8 of quilting pat until piece measures 9"/23cm from beg, end with a WS row.

BEGIN BAND FOR BACK OPENING
Next row (RS) With B, cast on 4 sts for band, [k1, p1] twice over these sts, work in quilting pat to end—67 sts. Cont in quilting pat and ribbed band until skirt measures 10"/25.5cm from

beg, end with a pat row 8. Place sts on holder.

RIGHT SIDE OF SKIRT
Work as for left side until piece measures 9"/23cm from beg, end with a RS row.
BEGIN BAND FOR BACK OPENING
Next row (WS) With B, cast on 4 sts for band, [p1, k1] twice over these sts, work in quilting pat to end—67 sts.
Cont in quilting pat and ribbed band until skirt measures 10"/25.5cm from beg, end with a row 8. Place sts on holder.

SKIRT INSERT
With C, cast on 30 sts. Rep rows 1–8 of tracks pat until piece measures 10"/25.5cm from beg, end with a WS row. AT THE SAME TIME, dec 1 st each side every 12th row 7 times—16 sts. Place sts on holder. Beg at center of the insert cast-on edge, with needle and thread run a 2"/5cm line of sts, pull gently to gather to create a scallop (see photo). Secure threads. Beg at cast-on edge and sew insert between skirts.

BODICE
Joining row 1 (RS) With B, rib 4 band sts from left skirt holder, k63, place marker (pm); with C, k16 from insert holder, pm; with 2nd ball of B, k63, rib 4 from right skirt holder—150 sts.
Row 2 (WS) With B, rib 4 sts, p1, [p2tog] 31 times, sl marker; with C, [p2tog] 8 times, sl marker; with B, [p2tog] 31 times, p1, rib 4 sts—36 sts in B on each side, 8 sts in C in center.
Rows 3–6 Cont in established colors and work even in St st.
Color shift row 7 (RS) With B, rib 4 sts, knit to 2 sts before marker, k2tog, sl marker; with C, CO1, knit to marker, CO1, sl marker; with B, k2tog, knit to last 4 sts, rib 4 sts—35 sts on each side, 10 sts in C in center.
Cont as established and rep row 7 for color shift every 4th row twice more—33 sts on each side, 14 sts in center. Work even until bodice measures 2"/5cm from joining row, end with a WS row.

DIVIDE FOR FRONT AND BACK
Next row (RS) With B, rib 4 sts, k16,

place these sts on holder for left back; bind off 4 sts for left armhole; knit to marker, sl marker, with C, knit to marker, sl marker, with C, k9, place these sts on holder for front; bind off 4 sts for right armhole; k to end—20 sts for right back.

RIGHT BACK
Cont in St st with ribbed band on 20 sts for right back until armhole measures 1"/2.5cm, end with a RS row.
Next row (WS) Bind off 12 sts for neck, purl to end—8 sts.
Work even in St st until armhole measures 2"/5cm. Bind off.

LEFT BACK
Sl sts to needle ready for a WS row. Rejoin B and cont in St st with ribbed band until armhole measures 1"/2.5cm, end with a WS row.
Next row (RS) Bind off 12 sts for neck, knit to end—8 sts.
Work even in St st until armhole measures 2"/5cm. Bind off.

FRONT
Rejoin yarn to 32 front sts ready to work a WS row. Work in St st and established colors for ½"/1.5cm, end with a WS row.

SHAPE NECK
Row 1 (RS) With B, k7, k2tog, sl marker; with C, CO1, k14, CO1, sl marker; with B, k2tog, k to end—8 sts on each side, 16 sts in center.
Rows 2–4 Cont in St st and established colors.
Row 5 With B, k to marker, remove marker; with C, bind off 16 sts purlwise, and fasten off, remove marker; with B, k to end. Work even in St st on 8 sts each side until front armholes measure 2"/5cm. Bind off.

SLEEVES
With B, cast on 54 sts.
Knit 4 rows.
Beg with a RS row, work 8 rows in St st.
Dec row (RS) [K2tog] 27 times—27 sts. Purl 3 rows. Cut yarn.
Inc row (RS) With C, [kfb] 27 times—54 sts.
Work even in St st until sleeve measures 4"/10cm from beg, end with a WS row.

SHAPE SLEEVE CAP
Bind off 2 sts at beg of next 2 rows—50 sts. Knit 1 row, purl 1 row.
Dec row (RS) K1, [k3tog] 16 times, k1—18 sts. Bind off.

BODICE LACING
With crochet hook and B, chain 18"/45.5cm long and fasten off. Using photo as guide, beg and end at bodice, join and lace the chain through the center of bodice, forming two X's. Secure with knots on WS.

FINISHING
Sew shoulder seams. Sew sleeve seams. Sew sleeves to armholes. Thread elastic through sleeve dec row on WS. Tack down edges of ribbed bands to skirt. Sew 4 snaps evenly to ribbed bands.

LEFT SIDE EDGING
With circular needle, A and RS facing, beg at back left neck and skip ribbed band, pick up and k 10 sts to shoulder seam; pick up and k 100 sts along front edge of left skirt only, from shoulder seam to cast-on edge, picking up sts from skirt side, not insert; pick up and k 52 sts along cast-on edge of left skirt—162 sts. Bind off.

RIGHT SIDE EDGING
Work in same manner as left side, pick up and k 52 sts along cast-on edge of right skirt; pick up and knit 100 sts along front edge of right skirt only, from cast-on edge to shoulder seam; pick up and k 12 sts along back shoulder and neck edge including ribbed band—164 sts. Bind off. Sew back skirt seam.

HAT
With A, cast on 73 sts. Knit 2 rows.
Row 1 (WS) With A, k1, p1, [sl 9 wyib, p1] 7 times, k1.
Row 2 With B, knit.
Row 3 With B, k1, purl to last st, k1.
Rows 4–7 Rep rows 2 and 3 twice.
Row 8 With A, k1, sl 4 wyib, [LD, sl 7 wyib] 6 times, LD, sl 4 wyib, k1—59 sts.
Row 9 With A, k1, sl 4 wyib, [p1, sl 7 wyib] 6 times, p1, sl 4 wyib, k1.
Rows 10–15 With B, rep rows 2 and 3 three times.

Row 16 With A, k1, [CS, sl 7 wyib] 7 times, CS, k1.
Row 17 With A, k1, p1, [sl 7 wyib, p1] 7 times, k1.
Rows 18–23 Rep rows 2 and 3 three times.
Row 24 With A, k1, sl 3 wyib, [LD, sl 5 wyib] 6 times, LD, sl 3 wyib, k1—45 sts.
Row 25 With A, k1, sl 3 wyib, [p1, sl 5 wyib] 6 times, p1, sl 3 wyib, k1.
Rows 26–31 Rep rows 2 and 3 three times.
Row 32 With A, k1, [CS, sl 5 wyib] 7 times, CS, k1.
Row 33 With A, k1, p1, [sl 5 wyib, p1] 7 times, k1.
Row 34–39 Rep rows 2 and 3 three times.
Row 40 With A, k1, sl 2 wyib, [LD, sl 3 wyib] 6 times, LD, sl 2 wyib, k1—31 sts.
Row 41 With A, k1, sl 2 wyib, [p1, sl 3 wyib] 6 times, p1, sl 2 wyib, k1.
Rows 42–47 Rep rows 2 and 3 three times.
Row 48 With A, k1, [CS, sl 3 wyib] 7 times, CS, k1.
Row 49 With A, k1, p1, [sl 3 wyib, p1] 7 times, k1.
Rows 50–55 Rep rows 2 and 3 three times.
Row 56 With A, k1, sl 1 wyib, [LD, sl 1 wyib] 6 times, LD, sl 1 wyib, k1—17 sts.
Row 57 With A, k1, purl to last st, k1.
Row 58 With A, k1, [k2tog 8 times—9 sts.

FINISHING

Cut yarn, leaving a long tail. Thread through open sts and pull tight. Don't cut tail. Block flat. Sew seam.

PAPER HAT INSERT
Make copy of template (page 117), enlarging at 5 percent. Place manila folder or stiff paper on copy, trace, and cut out. Wrap to form cone and secure edges with tape. Brush cone lightly with glue. Starting at top point, place knit hat over cone, pull yarn tail through top of hat and secure inside with tape.
Cut 2 pieces of tulle each approx 5"/12.5cm wide x 14"/36 long. Place the 2 pieces together, gather at one short end and sew to top of hat.

HAIR BRAID

Open hank of D and cut loops open at one end. Tie off other end securely. Divide yarn into three sections and braid, tie end with D to secure. Weave E through braid. Attach to inside of hat. ✳

Peter Pan

●●●○

"Doesn't Peter Pan Look Grand Flying Off to Neverland?"

MATERIALS
- 1 3½oz/100g skein (each approx 175yd/156m) of Lion Brand *Vanna's Choice* (acrylic) in #172 kelly green (A) **4**
- 1 bag of *Vanna's Palettes in #207 spirited*: 8 mini skeins in colors including bright chartreuse (B), chartreuse (C), seafoam green (F), olive green (D), and warm medium brown (E) **4**
- One pair size 4 (3.5mm) needles OR SIZE TO OBTAIN GAUGE
- Size E/4 (3.5mm) crochet hook
- One 6"/15cm red feather for cap
- 3 snaps
- 8 stitch markers
- 2 removable stitch markers
- 2 stitch holders
- 1½"/4cm belt buckle (a watchband buckle will also work)
- Narrow strips of leather for wrists
- Sewing needle and thread

GAUGE
20 sts and 26 rows to 4"/10cm over St st using size 4 (3.5mm) needles. TAKE TIME TO CHECK GAUGE.

STITCH GLOSSARY
CO1 (cast on 1—increase) Wrap yarn around left thumb from back to front. Insert RH needle from front into loop on thumb. Remove thumb from loop and tighten loop on needle (also called wrap cast-on). 1 stitch increased.

NOTE
The tunic begins with 6 points that are each knit separately, then joined.

TUNIC
POINTS (make 6)
With A, cast on 2 sts.
*Row 1 (RS) K1, CO1, k1—3 sts.
Row 2 and all WS rows Purl.
Row 3 K1, CO1, k1, CO1, k1—5 sts.
Row 5 K1, CO1, k3, CO1, k1—7 sts.
Row 7 K1, CO1, k5, CO, k1—9 sts.
Row 9 K1, CO1, k7, CO1, k1—11 sts.
Cut yarn and leave sts on needle. Cast on 2 sts onto separate needle, then work row 1 onto needle with other point(s), and rep from * 5 more times—6 points on 1 needle.
Do *not* cut yarn at end of sixth point.
Joining row (WS) P66.
Inc row (RS) K1, CO1, knit to last st, CO1, k1—68 sts.
Work even in St st (knit on RS, purl on WS) until piece measures 3"/7.5cm from joining row, end with a RS row.

BEGIN SHAPING
Set-up row (WS) [P12, place marker (pm), p1, pm] twice, p16, [pm, p1, pm, p12] twice.
Dart row (RS) [K to 2 sts before marker, ssk, sl marker, k1, sl marker, k2tog] 4 times, k to end—8 sts dec'd. Purl 1 row. Rep last 2 rows once more—52 sts.

Remove shaping markers, place 1 removable marker at each end of last row. Work even in St st until piece measures 5¼"/13.5cm from joining row, end with a WS row.

DIVIDE FOR FRONT AND BACK
Next row (RS) K12 for left back and sl to holder, bind off 2 sts for left armhole, k until there are 24 sts on RH needle and sl to holder for front, bind off 2 sts for right armhole, k to end—12 sts for right back.

RIGHT BACK
Work even in St st on 12 right back sts until armhole measures 2½"/6.5cm, end with a WS row. Bind off.

LEFT BACK
Place 12 left back sts on needle, ready for a WS row. Rejoin A.
Work even in St st until armhole measures 2½"/6.5cm, end with a WS row. Bind off.

FRONT
Place 24 front sts on needle, ready for a WS row. Rejoin A.
Work even in St st until armhole measures 1½"/4cm, end with a WS row.

SHAPE NECK
Next row (RS) K9, join a 2nd ball of A and bind off center 6 sts, knit to end—9 sts each side of neck.
Next row (WS) Purl across each side

Row 11 SK2P.
Fasten off rem st.

FINISHING

With RS tog, fold tunic, matching first and last points. Sew back seam from markers to beg of points. Remove markers.
With RS tog, starting at armhole edge, sew 8 bound-off sts of left shoulders tog, leaving last 4 bound-off sts of back free for back neck. Rep for right shoulder.
Sew sleeve seams. Set in sleeves.
With A and crochet hook, work 1 row of sc along edges of back opening for bands.
Sew 2 snaps to center and top of bands.
Sew 12 leaves to neck edge, using photo as guide.

BELT

With E, cast on 7 sts.
Row 1 (RS) *K1, p1; rep from *, end k1.
Row 2 P1, *k1, p1; rep from * to end.
Rep rows 1 and 2 for k1, p1 rib until belt measures 11"/28cm from beg.
Bind off.
Slide buckle to center of belt. Sew snap to ends.

HAT

With A, cast on 66 sts.
Work in St st for 2 rows.
Dec row (RS) K1, ssk, knit to last 3 sts, k2tog, k1—2 sts dec'd.
Cont in St st, rep dec row every other row 4 more times, end with a RS row—56 sts.

SHAPE TOP
Set-up row (WS) P27, pm, p2, pm, p27.
Dec row (RS) K1, ssk, knit to 2 sts before marker, ssk, sl marker, k2, sl marker, k2tog, k to last 3 sts, k2tog, k1—4 sts dec'd.
Cont in St st and rep dec row every other row 9 more times—16 sts.
Purl 1 row.
Dec row (RS) K1, ssk, [k2tog] 6 times, k1—9 sts.
Dec row (WS) P1, [p2tog] 4 times—5 sts.
Pass the 2nd, 3rd, 4th, and 5th sts one at a time over first st. Fasten off.

ANGLED BRIM
With RS tog, fold hat along center decs.
Sew side edges tog, beg at cast-on row.
Turn RS out. Fold cast-on edge up on RS

---

of neck.
Dec row Knit across left side of neck to last 2 sts, k2tog; on right side of neck ssk, knit to end—8 sts rem each side for shoulder.
Work even in St st until armhole measures 2½"/6.5cm, end with a WS row.
Bind off.

SLEEVES (make 2)
With A, cast on 21 sts.
Work in St st until sleeve measures 1½"/4cm from beg, end with a WS row.

SHAPE SLEEVE CAP
Bind off 2 sts at beg of next 2 rows, then bind off 1 st at beg of next 2 rows—15 sts.
Work even until 1"/2.5cm above first

bind-off, end with a WS row.
Dec 1 st each side on next row, then every other row twice more—9 sts.
Purl 1 row.
Dec row (RS) [K2tog] twice, k1, [k2tog] twice—5 sts.
Bind off purlwise.

LEAVES

(make 16: 6 with B, 7 with C, 3 with D)
Cast on 5 sts.
Row 1 (RS) K2, yo, k1, yo, k2—7 sts.
Row 2 and all WS rows Purl.
Row 3 K3, yo, k1, yo, k3—9 sts.
Row 5 Ssk, k5, k2tog—7 sts.
Row 7 Ssk, k3, k2tog—5 sts.
Row 9 Ssk, k1, k2tog—3 sts.

for ¼"/.5cm at seam, and for 1"/2.5cm at center decs, forming angled brim. Sew cast-on edge in place. Push end of feather in and out through side of hat, using photo as guide for placement.

BOOTS (make 2)
With A, cast on 46 sts.
Work in St st for 2 rows.
Dec row (RS) K1, ssk, k to last 3 sts, k2tog, k1—2 sts dec'd.
Purl 1 row.
Rep last 2 rows twice more—40 sts.
Dec row (RS) K1, [ssk] 3 times, k to last 7 sts, [k2tog] 3 times, k1—6 sts dec'd.
Purl 1 row.
Rep last 2 rows twice more—22 sts.
Cut A.
With F, work even in St st for 4 rows.
Picot bind-off (RS) Bind off 2 sts, *sl st on RH needle to LH needle, cast on 3 sts, then bind off 5 sts; rep from * 9 more times—10 picots.
Fasten off.
With RS tog, fold boot in half. Beg at last row of A working toward cast-on edge, sew side edges tog for front of boot, then seam along cast-on row for bottom of foot. Turn RS out. Sew 1 B leaf and 1 C leaf to first row of F on opposite sides to designate right and left foot, using photo as guide. ✳

Cinderella

●●●○

"She Lost Her Slipper With a Thump
She Should Have Worn a Low-Heeled Pump"

MATERIALS
- 3 .88oz/25g cones (each approx 108yd/100m) of Skacel *Vegas* (rayon/metallic polyester) in #11 light blue metallic (A) ❸
- 1 cone each in #04 white metallic (B) and #12 light gold metallic (C)
- One pair size 3 (3.25mm) needles OR SIZE TO OBTAIN GAUGE
- One size 3 (3.25mm) circular needle, 16"/40cm long
- 5 snaps
- 6 tiny pearl beads
- Sewing needle and thread
- Stitch markers and holders
- 30"/76cm costume jewelry gold chain for waist belt (optional)
- 7 costume jewels for crown: 4 diamond, 3 sapphire
- 13"/33cm of ¼"/.5cm blue satin ribbon for crown

GAUGE
28 sts and 40 rows to 4"/10cm over St st (knit on RS, purl on WS) using size 3 (3.25mm) needles.
TAKE TIME TO CHECK GAUGE.

STITCH GLOSSARY
Pfb Purl into the front and back of st to inc 1 st.

NOTE
See page 122 for sewing instructions for crinoline.

DIAMOND BROCADE PATTERN
(multiple of 8 sts plus 1)
Row 1 (RS) K4, *p1, k7; rep from * to last 5 sts, p1, k4.
Row 2 P3, *k1, p1, k1, p5; rep from * to last 3 sts, p3.
Row 3 K2, *p1, k3; rep from * to last 3 sts, p1, k2.
Row 4 P1, *k1, p5, k1, p1; rep from * to end.
Row 5 *P1, k7; rep from * to last st, p1.
Row 6 Rep row 4.
Row 7 Rep row 3.
Row 8 Rep row 2.
Rep rows 1–8 for diamond brocade pat.

GOWN
With B, cast on 129 sts.
Work 4 rows in St st.
Picot row (RS) K1, *yo, k2tog; rep from * to end.
Work 4 rows in St st.
Change to A and purl 1 row on WS.

BEGIN DIAMOND BROCADE PAT
Work in diamond brocade pat until skirt measures 9"/23cm from picot row, end with a WS row.
Dec row (RS) K3, [k2tog] 62 times, k2—67 sts.
Purl 1 row.

BODICE
Row 1 (RS) Cast on 4 sts, [k1, p1] twice over these 4 sts, k to end—71 sts.
Row 2 (WS) Cast on 4 sts, [p1, k1] twice over these 4 sts, p to last 4 sts, work in established rib to end—75 sts.
Cont in St st keeping first and last 4 sts in rib for bands until bodice measures 2"/5cm.

DIVIDE FOR FRONT AND BACKS
Next row (RS) Work 18 sts in pat and place these sts on holder for left back, bind off 3 sts for left armhole, knit until there are 33 sts on needle and slip to holder for front, bind off 3 sts for right armhole, work to end—18 sts for right back.

RIGHT BACK
Work even until armhole measures 2½"/6.5cm. Bind off.

LEFT BACK
Sl 18 sts to needle and join B, ready to work a WS row.
Work even until armhole measures 2½"/6.5cm. Bind off.

FRONT
Sl 33 sts on needle and join B, ready to work a WS row. Work even in St st until armholes measure 1"/2.5cm.

SHAPE NECK
Next row (RS) K12 for left neck and sl to holder, join a 2nd ball of B and bind off center 9 sts, k to end—12 sts for right neck.

RIGHT NECK
Row 1 (WS) Purl.
Row 2 (RS) Ssk, knit to end—11 sts.
Rep rows 1 and 2 once more—10 sts.
Work even until armhole measures 2½"/6.5cm. Bind off.

LEFT NECK
Sl 12 sts back to needle, ready for a WS row.
Row 1 (WS) Purl.
Row 2 (RS) K to last 2 sts, k2tog—11 sts.
Rep rows 1 and 2 once more—10 sts.

Work even until armhole measures 2½"/6.5cm. Bind off.

BODICE DETAIL
Count down 28 rows from center front neck bind-off and place a marker on the center st. With B, work duplicate st and attach pearl beads following chart (work the first duplicate st on row 1 at the center marked st). Rep rows 1–8 of chart 3 times, then rep row 1 to neck bind-off.

SLEEVES
With A, cast on 12 sts.
Row 1 (RS) K1, [kfb] 10 times, k1—22 sts.
Row 2 Purl.
Row 3 *K1, kfb; rep from * to end—33 sts.
Row 4 Purl to end, CO1—34 sts.
Rows 5–12 Work even in St st.

BEGIN COLOR PATTERN
Row 13 (RS) [K2 A, k2 B] 8 times, k2 A.
Row 14 [P2 A, p2 B] 8 times, p2 A.
Rows 15–20 Rep rows 13 and 14 three more times.
Row 21 (RS) With A, k1, [k2tog] 16 times, k1—18 sts.
Row 22 Purl.
Row 23 [K1, k2tog] 6 times—12 sts. Bind off.

FINISHING
Sew shoulder seams.

NECK BAND
With circular needle, B and RS facing, pick up and k 44 sts evenly along neck edge.
Work in rev St st (purl on RS, knit on WS) for ½"/1.5cm. Bind off. Band will roll to WS. Tack in place.
Sew back seam of skirt. Sew 4 snaps evenly spaced to back opening. Fold sleeves in half with WS tog and sew cast-on edge to bound-off edge. With color pattern facing, sew sleeve seam to top of armhole, centering at shoulder (see photo).

BUSTLE (make 2 pieces)
With B, cast on 15 sts.

Row 1 (RS) Kfb, knit to last st, kfb—17 sts.
Row 2 Pfb, purl to last st, pfb—19 sts.
Rows 3–10 Rep rows 1 and 2 four more times—35 sts.
Cont in St st and rep row 1 every RS row 3 more times, then every 4th row 2 more times—45 sts.
Work 6 rows even in St st.
Place sts on a holder.

EDGING
With circular needle, C and RS facing, pick up and k 70 sts evenly along cast-on edge and sides of one piece. Knit 1 row. Bind off. Repeat for second piece.

JOIN BUSTLE PIECES
Place both bustle pieces on same needle ready to work a RS row.
Joining row 1 (RS) With C, on first bustle: *pick up and k 2 sts on side of edging, then from needle k1, [k2tog] 22 times, pick up and k 2 sts along side of edging; rep from * with same yarn on 2nd bustle—54 sts.
Row 2 (WS) Cast on 6 sts, k to end—60 sts.
Row 3 Cast on 6 sts, k to end—66 sts.
Rows 4-6 Knit.
Bind off.
Sew snap to ends of top edging. See photo for example, and with needle and sewing thread, run 1"/2.5cm of sts through center of each piece starting at cast-on edge. Pull gently to gather, secure thread. Attach chain to center front of waist as shown in photo if desired.

CROWN
With C, cast on 8 sts.
Row 1 (RS) Knit.
Row 2 Sl 1, k2, yo, k2tog, k1, [yo] 4 times, k2—12 sts.
Row 3 Sl 1, k1, (drop 3 yos to make 1 long st, [k1, p1] twice into that st), k3, yo, k2tog, k1—12 sts.
Row 4 Sl 1, k2, yo, k2tog, k7.
Row 5 Sl 1, k8, yo, k2tog, k1.
Row 6 Sl 1, k2, yo, k2tog, k7.
Row 7 Bind off 4 sts, yo, k4, k2tog, k1—8 sts.
Rep rows 2–7 eighteen more times or

until crown fits around your doll's head, end with a row 7.
Bind off all sts purlwise. Sew cast-on and bound-off edges together. Decorate front of crown with jewels. Thread blue ribbon through yo's at end of RS rows. Use photo as a guide.

GAUNTLETS (make 2)
With B, cast on 29 sts.
Row 1 (RS) Knit.
Row 2 Purl.
Rows 3–6 Work in St st.
Row 7 (RS) Ssk, knit to last 2 sts, k2tog—27 sts.
Row 8 Purl.
Rows 9–12 Work in St st.
Row 13 Rep row 7—25 sts.
Rows 14–18 Work in St st.
Row 19 Rep row 7—23 sts.
Work even until piece measures 2½"/6.5cm from beg, end with a WS row.

SHAPE POINT
Bind off 4 sts at beg of next 2 rows—15 sts.
Row 1 (RS) K1, ssk, k to last 3 sts, k2tog, k1—13 sts.
Row 2 Purl.
Rows 3–10 Rep last 2 rows 4 more times—5 sts.
Row 11 (RS) K1, SK2P, k1—3 sts.
Row 12 P1, p2tog, pass the p1 over the p2tog and fasten off.
With WS facing, fold gauntlet in half, seam edges tog from cast-on edge to bound-off sts.✻

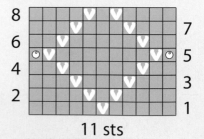

11 sts

KEY

⊽ duplicate stitch in B

⊙ attach pearl

Noble Unicorn

*"Behold the Noble Unicorn
She Is Content With Just One Horn"*

MATERIALS
- 1 1¾oz/50g skein (each approx 202yd/185m) of Lion Brand *Vanna's Glamour* (acrylic/metallic polyester) each in #100 diamond (A) and 171 gold (B) [2]
- 1 1¾oz/50g skein (each approx 27yd/25m) of Lion Brand *Romance* (nylon/polyester) in #100 silky white (C) [6]
- 1 1¾oz/50g cone (each approx 143yd/131m) of Skacel *Karat* (polyester metallic) in #04 light gold metallic (D) [4]
- One pair each sizes 3 and 6 (3.25 and 4mm) needles OR SIZE TO OBTAIN GAUGE
- Size 3 (3.25mm) double-pointed needles (dpns)
- 5 layers of poly-fil stuffing, approx 7 x 18"/18 x 45.5cm each
- Polyester stuffing
- Sewing needle and thread
- Glue
- 2 small blue animal eyes
- Small amount of pink felt
- Stitch markers and holders
- 24"/61cm gray satin ribbon, ¼"/.5cm wide
- 2 pink beads or buttons for bridle

GAUGE
24 sts and 30 rows to 4"/10cm over St st in the rnd (knit every rnd) using smaller needles and A. TAKE TIME TO CHECK GAUGE.

NOTE
When working with C, be sure to insert needle completely into st to avoid dropping sts. This yarn is very slippery.

BODY
With larger needles and A, cast on 69 sts.
Row 1 (RS) *K1, kfb; rep from * to last st, k1—103 sts.
Cont in St st until piece measures 5½"/14cm from beg.
Last row (RS) *K1, k2tog; rep from * to last st, k1—69 sts. Bind off.
Roll the layers of poly-fil to form a tight tube and sew to secure. Cover tube with knitted piece and sew seam. Sew cast-on and bound-off ends of tube tog, being sure that long seam is on inside of tube.

HEAD
Note Head is worked from neck to nose. With smaller dpns, cast on 36 sts and divide evenly over 3 needles—12 sts on each needle. Join, being careful not to twist sts, and place marker (pm) for beg of rnd.
[Knit 1 rnd, purl 1 rnd] twice.
Work in St st (knit every rnd) until piece measures 1½"/4cm from beg.
Next rnd [K2tog, k10] 3 times—33 sts.
Work even until piece measures 3"/7.5cm from beg.
Next rnd [K2tog, k9] 3 times—30 sts.
Work even until piece measures 4½"/11.5cm from beg.

TOP OF HEAD
Redistribute sts as foll: k15, sl to holder and set aside; k15 sts to dpn for back neck, turn.
Work back and forth in rows over dpn as foll:
Row 1 (WS) P15.
Row 2 (RS) [K1, sl 1] 7 times, k1.
Rows 3–6 Rep rows 1 and 2 twice.

BEG SHORT ROWS
Row 7 (WS) P9, p2tog, p1, turn—11 sts on dpn, 3 sts rem unworked.
Row 8 Sl 1, k4, ssk, k1, turn.
Row 9 Sl 1, p5, p2tog, p1, turn.
Row 10 Sl 1, k6, ssk, k1, turn.
Row 11 Sl 1, p6, p2tog, p1, turn.
Row 12 Sl 1, k6, ssk, k1—9 sts on dpn. Do *not* turn.
Joining rnd (RS) With dpn #2, pick up and k 5 sts along side edge of short rows, k 7 sts from holder—12 sts for left side of head; with dpn #3, k rem 8 sts from holder, pick up and k 4 sts along other side edge of short rows—12 sts for right side of head; join to work in rnds, pm for beg of rnd, and with dpn #1, work rem 9 sts for top of head—33 sts.
Work in rnds of St st until 2"/5cm above joining rnd.

NOSE/MOUTH
Rnd 1 (RS) Dpn #1: ssk, k to last 2 sts, k2tog—7 sts; dpn #2: k2, ssk, k to end—11 sts; dpn #3: k to last 4 sts, k2tog, k2—11 sts.
Rnd 2 Knit.
Rnds 3–6 Rep rnd 1 and 2 twice—dpn #1—3 sts; dpns #2 and #3—9 sts each.
Rnd 7 Dpn #1: S2KP—1 st; dpn #2: k2, ssk, k to end—8 sts; dpn #3: k to last 4 sts, k2tog, k2—8 sts.
Rnd 8 Knit.
Cut yarn, leaving long tail. With yarn needle, thread tail through 17 rem sts and pull tightly.

LEGS (MAKE 4)
HOOF
With smaller needles and B, cast on 12 sts.

Row 1 (RS) Kfb in each st across—24 sts.
Rows 2–16 Knit (8 ridges).
Row 17 [K2, k2tog] 6 times—18 sts. Cut B.

LEG

With A, beg with a p row on WS, work in St st for 2¼"/5.5cm, end with a WS row.
Inc row (RS) *K1, kfb; rep from * to end—27 sts.
Work even in St st for 1"/2.5cm, end with a WS row.
Dec row (RS) *K1, k2tog; rep from * to end—18 sts.
Work even in St st for 3"/7.5cm. Bind off.

HOOF FRINGE (MAKE 4)

With larger needles and C, cast on 20 sts. Knit 1 row. Bind off.

EARS

With smaller needles and A, cast on 6 sts.
Inc row (RS) Kfb in each st across—12 sts.
Work even in St st until piece measures ½"/1.5cm from beg, end with a WS row.
Dec row (RS) K1, ssk, k6, k2tog, k1—10 sts.
Rep dec row every RS row 3 more times—4 sts.
Purl 1 row on WS.
Next row Ssk, k2tog—2 sts.
Last row P2tog. Fasten off.

HORN

With dpns and D, cast on 10 sts. Divide sts evenly over 3 needles (3 – 4 – 3). Join, being careful not to twist sts, and pm for beg of rnd.
Rnd 1 Purl.
Rnd 2 [Kfb] 10 times around—20 sts.
Rnds 3–7 Knit.
Rnd 8 (ridge) [P2tog] 10 times around—10 sts.
Rnd 9 [K1, kfb] 5 times around—15 sts.
Rnds 10–14 Knit.
Rnd 15 [P2tog] 7 times, p1—8 sts.
Rnd 16 [Kfb, k2] twice, kfb, k1—11 sts.
Rnds 17–20 Knit.
Rnd 21 [P2tog] 5 times, p1—6 sts.

Rnds 22–26 Knit.
Rnd 27 [K2tog] 3 times—3 sts.
Rnd 28 SK2P. Fasten off.

MANE

Loop stitch: Insert needle in a st, wrap yarn over RH needle knitwise, them over 2, 3, or 4 fingers of left hand and over RH needle again (there are 2 loops on needle), draw both loops through the st, insert LH needle into fronts of these 2 loop and k them tog through back loops.
With larger needles and C, cast on 16 sts.
Row 1 K1, [work loop st in next st over 2 fingers] 4 times, [work loop st in next st over 3 fingers] 6 times, [work loop st in next st over 4 fingers] 5 times.
Row 2 Knit. Bind off.

FINISHING

HEAD

Stuff head and neck with polyester filling, sew to side of body ring. Using template on page TK, cut 2 felt pieces to fit into ears, sew or glue in place on WS of ear. Sew ears in place on head, using photo as a guide. Sew or glue eyes in place. Cut 2 small felt circles for nostrils and glue in place. Stuff horn and sew to center of head. Sew mane to back of neck.

BRIDLE
Cut length of ribbon to fit around horse's nose, sew in place, using photo as guide. Cut rem ribbon in half, sew each piece in place as a rein. Sew one pink bead on top of both rein joins.

LEGS
Sew leg seams and stuff with polyester filling, arrange around ring, sew bound-off edge of each leg to bottom of ring. Sew fringe around legs at top of hooves.

I-CORD TAIL
With dpns and A, cast on 5 sts, *k5, slide sts to opposite end of needle to work next row from RS, pulling yarn tightly across back of work. Rep from * until cord measures 1½"/4cm from beg.
Next rnd K2tog, k1, k2tog—3 sts. Slide to opposite end of needle. Change to larger dpns and C.
Next row (RS) Make a loop st in each of 3 rem sts as for mane, wrapping 3 times around 4 fingers for each st. Bind off. With C, make a tassel and attach with a long loop to the end of the I-cord. Sew cast-on edge of tail to outside of body ring, opposite the head. ✳

Child's Unicorn Hood

Kids can make their own magic with this fun hood!

●●●○

FINISHED MEASUREMENTS
Instructions are written for one size.
Hood at widest point approx 14"/35.5cm
Hood length approx 15"/38cm

MATERIALS
- 3 1¾oz/50g balls (each approx 27yd/25m) of Lion Brand *Romance* (nylon/polyester) in #100 silky white (A) (6)
- 1 1¾oz/50g cone (each approx 143yd/131m) of Skacel *Karat* (polyester

metallic) in #04 light gold metallic (B) (4)
- 1 3½oz/100g skein (each approx 175yd/156m) of Lion Brand *Vanna's Choice* (acrylic) in #100 white (C) (4)
- One pair size 8 (5mm) needles OR SIZE TO OBTAIN GAUGE
- **One pair each** sizes 2 and 4 (2.75 and 3.5mm) needles
- Yarn needle
- Small amount of polyester stuffing
- 4 x 6"/10 x 15cm piece of pink felt fabric

- Glue
- Sewing needle and thread

GAUGE
12 sts to 4"/10cm over St st using size 8 (5mm) needles and A. Row gauge does not matter. Fabric will stretch over time. TAKE TIME TO CHECK GAUGE.

FUR HOOD
Note This yarn can be slippery; be sure to insert needle completely into st to avoid dropping it.
With size 8 (5mm) needles and A, cast on 102 sts.
Row 1 (RS) K1, k2tog, k to last 3 sts, k2tog, k1—100 sts.
Row 2 P1, p2tog, p to last 3 sts, p2tog, p1—98 sts.
Rows 3–12 Rep rows 1 and 2 for 5 times—78 sts.
Work even in St st (k on RS, p on WS) until piece measures 7"/18cm from beg. Bind off loosely and fasten off last st securely. Mark "fluffier" side as RS. With RS tog, fold hood in half lengthwise and sew the bound-off edge for back seam.

HORN
With size 4 (3.5mm) needles and B, cast on 32 sts.
Rows 1–12 Beg with a knit row, work in St st.
Row 13 (RS) K1, [k2tog] 15 times, k1—17 sts.
Row 14 (WS) With size 2 (2.75mm) needles, knit.
Row 15 With size 4 (3.5mm) needles, [k1, kfb] 8 times, k1—25 sts.

Rows 16–22 Beg with a purl row, work in St st.
Row 23 (RS) K1, [k2tog] 12 times—13 sts.
Row 24 (WS) With size 2 (2.75mm) needles, knit.
Row 25 With size 4 (3.5mm) needles, k1, [kfb, k2] 4 times—17 sts.
Rows 26–30 Beg with a purl row, work in St st.
Row 31 (RS) K1, [k2tog] 8 times—9 sts.
Row 32 (WS) With size 2 (2.75mm) needles, knit.
Rows 33–36 With size 4 (3.5mm) needles, work in St st.
Row 37 (RS) K1, ssk, k to last 3 sts, k2tog, k1—7 sts.
Row 38 Purl.
Rows 39 and 40 Rep rows 37 and 38—5 sts.
Row 41 K1, SK2P, k1—3 sts.
Row 42 Sl 1, p2tog, psso. Fasten off last st.

FINISHING
Sew side edges of horn tog for back seam. Fill the horn with stuffing, adding less at ridge rows and more in between to shape, as in photo.

EARS
With size 8 (5mm) needles and C, cast on 10 sts.
Row 1 (RS) K1, [kfb] 8 times, k1—18 sts.
Row 2 Purl.
Rows 3–6 Work in St st.
Row 7 (RS) K1, ssk, k to last 3 sts, k2tog, k1—16 sts.
Row 8 Purl.
Rows 9–20 Rep rows 7 and 8 for 6 times—4 sts.
Row 21 (RS) K1, k2tog, k1—3 sts.
Row 22 Sl 1, p2tog, psso. Fasten off last st.

INNER EARS
Using template on page 116, cut 2 pieces of felt to fit into rev St st side of ears, then sew or glue in place.

ASSEMBLY
Using photo as guide, center horn on top of hood at approx 1½"/4cm from front edge. Sew in place. Sew ears to each side at approx 3"/8cm from front edge. ✳

A RECIPE FROM NICKY

Magic Star Wands

MAKES 12 STARS WITH WANDS

INGREDIENTS
1 15 x 12 x 1 super sheet (32oz/907g) Rice Krispies Treats (or make your own from Rice krispies cereal)*
1 package (12oz/340.2g) candy wafers, white
⅓ package candy wafers, pink

Small soft paintbrush
Microwaveable bowl
3½" star cookie cutter
12 long decorative sticks
24 12" strands of colored ribbons
1 bottle of edible dust in silver or gold (optional)
Pastry brush

DIRECTIONS
1. Lay the Rice Krispies sheet on a flat surface and use the star cookie cutter to cut out 12 stars. Place the stars on a cookie sheet or waxed paper. Insert a stick into each star, between two of the star points.
2. Melt the white candy wafers in a bowl in the microwave. With the pastry brush, generously brush the melted wafers onto the face of each star. Refrigerate stars for candy coating to harden.
3. Remove stars from refrigerator and repeat the coating process on the back side of each star. With the small paintbrush, lightly brush the stars with edible gold dust if desired.
4. Melt the pink candy wafers. With a fork, drizzle the melted candy back and forth across each star on one side. Tie two strands of ribbon to the top of each straw.

*RICE KRISPIES TREATS:
1. In large saucepan, melt butter over low heat. Add marshmallows and stir until completely melted. Remove from heat.
2. Add KELLOGG'S RICE KRISPIES cereal. Stir until well coated.
3. Using buttered spatula or wax paper, evenly press mixture into 13 x 9 x 2-inch pan coated with cooking spray. Cool. Cut into 2-inch squares. Best if served the same day.

Microwave Directions:
In microwave-safe bowl, heat butter and marshmallows on high for 3 minutes, stirring after 2 minutes. Stir until smooth. Follow steps 2 and 3 above. Microwave cooking times may vary.

Fairy Godmother

●●●○

*"The Fairy Godmother Can Help You Wed
A Prince, a Duke, a Guy Named Fred"*

MATERIALS
- 2 .88oz/25g balls (each approx 137yd/125m) of Schulana *Kid-Paillettes* (kid mohair/polyester/silk) in #450 mauve (A) **1**
- 1 ball in #310 white (B)
- One pair each sizes 4 and 7 (3.5 and 4.5mm) needles OR SIZE TO OBTAIN GAUGE
- One spare size 7 (4.5mm) needle for 3-needle join
- 4 snaps
- Sewing needle and thread
- 5 removable stitch markers
- 2 stitch holders
- ½yd/.5m of ½"/1.5cm satin ribbon in pink
- 1yd/.9m of ¼"/.75cm ribbon with hanging beads
- ¼yd/.5m string of pink crystal beads
- 2 packages of 6 small pink bows by Offray
- Purchased wings and crown
- ½yd/.5m toile for cape
- 2 white satin roses for cape

GAUGES
20 sts and 26 rows to 4"/10cm over St st using larger needles and 1 strand of A.
22 sts and 28 rows to 4"/10cm over St st using smaller needles and 2 strands of A held tog.
TAKE TIME TO CHECK GAUGES.

K1, P1 RIB
(over an even number of sts)
Row 1 (RS) *K1, p1; rep from * to end.
Row 2 K the knit sts and p the purl sts.
Rep row 2 for k1, p1 rib.

3-NEEDLE JOIN
With RS of layers facing you and the needles parallel, *insert 3rd needle knitwise in the first st on each needle and knit them tog; rep from * until all sts are joined.

DRESS
INNER SKIRT LAYER
With larger needles and single strand of B, cast on 120 sts.
Knit 2 rows.
Work in St st (knit on RS, purl on WS) until piece measures 3½"/9cm from beg, end with a WS row. Cut yarn and leave sts on spare needle.

OUTER SKIRT LAYER
With larger needles and single strand of A, cast on 120 sts. Knit 2 rows.
Work in St st until piece measures 2½"/6.5cm from beg, end with a WS row.

JOIN LAYERS
Joining row (RS) With RS of both layers facing you and A, place outer layer on top of inner layer and join using 3-needle join—120 sts.
Cont in St st with A until outer layer measures 9¼"/23.5cm from beg, end with a WS row. Change to smaller needles.

SHAPE WAIST
Next row (RS) K2, [k2tog] 58 times, k2—62 sts.

BODICE
Note Bodice is worked on smaller needles with 2 strands held tog.
Next (dec) row (WS) Join 2nd strand of A and purl, dec 4 sts evenly across—58 sts.
Next row [K1, p1] twice, k to last 4 sts, [p1, k1] twice.
Working first and last 4 sts in k1, p1 rib as established, cont in St st over center 50 sts for 1¼"/3cm, end with a WS row.

DIVIDE FOR FRONT AND BACK
Next row (RS) Work 16 sts for left back and sl to holder, bind off 2 sts for left armhole, work until there are 22 sts on LH needle and sl to holder for front, bind off 2 sts for right armhole, work to end—16 sts for right back.

RIGHT BACK

Work even on 16 sts for right back until armhole measures ½"/1.25cm, end with a WS row. Change to 2 strands of B. Work even until armhole measures 2½"/6.5cm, end with a WS row. Bind off.

LEFT BACK

Place 16 left back sts on needle, ready for a WS row. Rejoin 2 strands A. Work even until armhole measures ½"/1.25cm, end with a WS row. Change to 2 strands of B. Work even until armhole measures 2½"/6.5cm, end with a WS row. Bind off.

FRONT

Place 22 front sts on needle, ready for a WS row. Rejoin 2 strands A. Purl next row on WS.

Next row (RS) Knit, dec 1 st each end—20 sts. Purl 1 row.
Join 2 strands B.

BEGIN COLOR PATTERN

Row 1 (RS) K2 B, k7 A, k2 B, k7 A, k2 B.
Row 2 P3 B, p5 A, p4 B, p5 A, p3 B.
Row 3 K4 B, k3 A, k6 B, k3 A, k4 B.
Cut A. Cont in St st with 2 strands of B

and cont in St st, inc 1 st each side on next row—22 sts. Work even until armhole measures 2"/6.5cm, end with a WS row.

NECK SHAPING

Next row (RS) K8 for left neck, join second 2 strands of B and bind off center 6 sts, knit to end for right neck—8 sts each side of neck.
Next row (WS) Purl across each side of neck.
Dec row Knit across left side of neck to last 2 sts, k2tog; on right side of neck, ssk, knit to end—7 sts rem each side. Working both sides of back at once with separate balls of yarn, rep last 2 rows once more—6 sts rem each side for shoulder. Work even in St st until armholes measure 2½"/6.5cm, end with a WS row. Bind off.

SLEEVES (make 2)

With smaller needles and 1 strand of A, cast on 25 sts. Knit 4 rows.
Work in St st, inc 1 st each side every 6th row 3 times—31 sts.
Work even until sleeve measures 3½"/9cm from beg, end with a WS row.

SHAPE SLEEVE CAP

Bind off 2 sts at beg of next 2 rows, dec 1 st each side *every* row twice—23 sts. Change to 1 strand B.
Next (inc) row (RS) K2, [kfb, k1] 9 times, kfb, k2—33 sts.
Work even for 1"/2.5cm.
Dec 1 st each side every other row 3 times—27 sts. Purl 1 row.
Next (dec) row (RS) [K3tog] 9 times—9 sts.
Purl 1 row. Bind off.

FINISHING

Sew shoulder seams.
With RS facing, smaller needles and 2 strands of B, pick up and k 42 sts along neck edge. Knit 4 rows. Bind off.
Sew sleeve seams. Set in sleeves, centering last dec row at shoulder seam.

RUCHED HEM

On top layer of skirt, place st marker at center front. Place markers at 4"/10cm and at 8"/20cm from marker on each side of center—5 markers.
Beg at center marker, with tapestry needle and A, attach yarn at joining row and weave down through column of sts to the cast-on row. Pull up tightly to gather, and secure to make ruche. Rep at all markers. Sew back seam of both skirt layers. Make final ruche at back seam. With sewing needle and thread, sew 4 snaps to ribbed back bands, evenly spaced.

EMBELLISHMENT

Working along lower edge of outer layer, sew one bow to each ruche, using photo as guide. Sew crystal beads around neckline. Sew a pink bow at center front neck below the beads. For ribbon belt, attach plain pink ribbon to end of beaded ribbon. Sew a pink bow at each end of beaded ribbon. Tie belt around waist.

CAPE

Cut toile to 18" x 20". Fold in half (fold is bottom hem). Sew top edges together with running stitch. Gather to 4"/10cm and secure threads. Sew beaded ribbon around fronts and back neck. Sew a rose to each side of front neck. ✳

Red Riding Hood

*"Miss Riding Hood Is Grandma Bound
I Hope the Wolf Is Not Around!"*

MATERIALS
- 2 1¾oz/50g balls (each approx 120yd/110m) of Rowan *Vanna's Chenille* (cotton) in #761 cardinal (A) (3)
- 1 1¾oz/50g ball (each approx 115yd/125m) of Rowan *Cotton Glace* (cotton) in #725 ecru (B) (3)
- 1 1¾oz/50g ball (each approx 125yd/137m) of Rowan *Purelife Revive* (cotton/silk/viscose) in #470 firestone (C) (3)
- One pair size 5 (3.75mm) needles OR SIZE TO OBTAIN GAUGE
- Size 5 (3.75mm) circular needle, 24"/60cm long
- 4 snaps
- 3 removable stitch markers
- 2 stitch holders
- 3 small decorative buttons
- 1yd/1m of ½"/1.5cm embroidered ribbon
- 24"/60cm of ¼"/.5cm red satin ribbon
- 1yd/1m of ¼"/.75cm fur strip (optional)
- Sewing needle and red thread

GAUGE
22 sts and 32 rows over St st using size 5 (3.75mm) needles and C. TAKE TIME TO CHECK GAUGE.

NOTE
Circular needle is needed to accommodate the number of sts worked for Riding Cape and Hood edging, but can be used on any piece if desired. There is no circular knitting in this pattern.

DRESS
With B, cast on 103 sts.
Work 4 rows in St st (knit on RS, purl on WS).
Picot row (RS) K1, *yo, k2tog; rep from * to end.
Work 4 more rows in St st. Cut B.
With C, cont in St st for 5"/12.5cm more, end with a WS row.
Dec row (RS) K3, [k2tog] 12 times, k1, [k2tog] 23 times, k1, [k2tog] 12 times, k4—56 sts.
Purl 1 row.

SHAPE BODICE
Inc row (RS) [K1, kfb] twice, k to last 4 sts, [kfb, k1] twice—60 sts.
Work even for 2"/5cm, end with a WS row.

DIVIDE FOR FRONT AND BACK
Next row (RS) K14 for left back and sl sts to holder, bind off 3 sts for left armhole, knit until there are 26 sts on RH needle and sl sts to holder for front, bind off 3 sts for right armhole, knit to end—14 sts for right back.

RIGHT BACK
Work even in St st on 14 right back sts until armhole measures 2½"/6.5cm, end with a WS row. Bind off.

LEFT BACK
Place 14 sts for left back on needle, ready for a WS row. Rejoin C.
Work even in St st until armhole measures 2½"/6.5cm, end with a WS row. Bind off.

FRONT
Place 26 sts for front on needle, ready for WS row. Rejoin C.
Work even in St st until armhole measures 1½"/4cm, end with a WS row.

SHAPE NECK
Next row (RS) K10, join a 2nd ball of C and bind off 6 sts, knit to end—10 sts each side of neck.
Next row (WS) Purl across each side of neck.
Dec row (RS) Knit across left side of neck to last 2 sts, k2tog; on right side of neck, ssk, knit to end—9 sts rem each side of neck. Rep last 2 rows once more—8 sts rem each side for shoulder.
Work even in St st until armhole measures 2½"/6.5cm, end with a WS row.
Bind off.

SLEEVES (make 2)
With B, cast on 25 sts. Knit 4 rows.
Inc row (RS) K1, [kfb] 23 times, k1—48 sts.
Work even in St st until sleeve measures 1¾"/4.5cm from beg, end with a WS row.

SHAPE SLEEVE CAP
Bind off 3 sts at beg of next 2 rows, then bind off 1 st at beg of next 2 rows—40 sts.
Work even until 1½"/4cm above first bind-off, end with a WS row.
Dec row (RS) K1, [k2tog] 5 times, [k3tog] 6 times, [k2tog] 5 times, k1—18 sts.
Dec row (WS) P1, [p3tog] 5 times, p2tog—7 sts.
Bind off.

COLLAR HALF (make 2)
With B, cast on 23 sts. Knit 6 rows. Bind off.

FINISHING
With RS tog, starting at armhole edge,

sew 8 bound-off sts of left shoulder tog, leaving last 6 sts of back free for back neck. Rep for right shoulder. Sew sleeve seams. Set sleeves into armholes. Mark center of front neck. Place collar halves between neck marker and side edges of neck. Sew to neck edge, using photo as guide. Remove marker.

With RS tog, sew center back seam from cast-on edge to 5"/12.5cm above picot row. Fold picot row to WS and sew cast-on edge to WS. Beg at waist and end at neck opening, sew four snaps evenly spaced to back opening. Sew buttons to center of front, using photo as guide.

APRON

With B, cast on 45 sts. Knit 6 rows. Work in St st until apron measures 4"/10cm from beg, end with a WS row.

Dec row (RS) [K2tog, k3tog] 9 times—18 sts.

Purl 1 row. Bind off.

Sew embroidered ribbon to bound-off edge of apron on RS, leaving approx 14"/35.5cm free on each side for ties.

RIDING CAPE AND HOOD

With A, cast on 98 sts. Knit 4 rows. Work in St st until piece measures 6"/15cm from beg, end with a WS row. Optional: sew fur around fronts and hood of cape with sewing thread.

SHAPE SHOULDERS

Row 1 (RS) With A, k1, [ssk, k12, k2tog] 6 times, k1—86 sts.

Row 2 and all WS rows Purl.

Row 3 K1, [ssk, k10, k2tog] 6 times, k1—74 sts.

Row 5 K1, [ssk, k8, k2tog] 6 times, k1—62 sts.

Row 7 K1, [ssk, k6, k2tog] 6 times, k1—50 sts.

Row 9 K1, [ssk, k4, k2tog] 6 times, k1—38 sts.

HOOD

Work even in St st on 38 sts for 5"/12.5cm more. Bind off. With RS tog, fold hood in half and sew bound-off edge tog to form hood top.

EDGING

With RS facing, circular needle and A, pick up and knit 156 sts evenly spaced up right front edge of cape, across hood, and down left front. Do not join. Knit 3 rows. Bind off. Cut satin ribbon in half and sew to both neck edges for front tie. ✱

Sleeping Beauty

●●●●

*"Sleeping Beauty Got Quite a Shock
When She Woke to an Alarm Clock"*

MATERIALS
- 1 1¾oz/50g skein (each approx 202yd/185m) of Lion Brand *Vanna's Glamour* (acrylic/metallc polyester) in #170 topaz (A), #146 jewel (B), and #195 rhinestone pink (C) (2)
- 1 .88oz/25g ball (each approx 109yd/100m) of Rowan *Anchor Artiste Metallic* (viscose/metallized polyester) in #300 gold (D) for crown (0)
- One pair each sizes 3 and 5 (3.25 and 3.75mm) needles OR SIZE TO OBTAIN GAUGE
- Spare sizes 3 and 5 (3.25 and 3.75mm) needles
- 1yd/1m of ⅛"/.5cm) pink ribbon
- Small cameo or jewel for neckband
- 4 small snaps
- 3 rhinestones or adornments for crown (optional)
- Stitch markers
- Stitch holders
- Scrap yarn
- 12"/30.5cm of light craft wire for crown

GAUGE
20 sts and 32 rows to 4"/10cm over St st (knit on RS, purl on WS) using larger needles and B or C. TAKE TIME TO CHECK GAUGE.

STITCH GLOSSARY
SP2P Sl 1, p2tog, pass slipped st over resulting st to dec 2 sts.

PROVISIONAL CAST-ON
Using scrap yarn and crochet hook, chain the number of sts to cast on, plus a few extra. Cut a tail and pull the tail through the last chain. With knitting needle and yarn, pick up and knit the stated number of sts through the "purl bumps" on the back of the chain. To remove scrap chain, when instructed, pull out the tail from the last crochet st. Gently and slowly pull on the tail to unravel the crochet sts, carefully placing each released knit st on a needle.

3-NEEDLE JOIN
With RS of layers facing you and the needles parallel, *insert 3rd needle knit-wise (or purlwise) in the first st on each needle and knit (or purl) them tog; rep from * until all sts are joined.

NOTE
1) Wind 4 balls each of B and C, approx 35yd/32m each, before beginning.
2) Skirt is worked using the intarsia technique. Use separate balls of yarn for each color section. Do not carry yarn across back of work.

GOWN
SKIRT
With A and larger needles, cast on 162 sts.
Row 1 (WS) P1, place marker (pm), k160, pm, p1.
Row 2 Knit, slipping markers.
Row 3 P1, sl marker (sm), knit to next marker, sm, p1.
Row 4 Rep row 2. Cut A.

BEGIN COLOR PAT
Set-up row (WS) With C, k1, sm, p20, [p20 B; p20 C] 3 times, with B, p20, sm, k1.
Row 1 (RS) With B, k1, sm, k20, [k20 C, k20 B] 3 times, with C, k20, sm, k1.
Work 3 rows more in St st and established colors.

BEGIN SHAPING
Cont in established colors and sl markers each row as foll:
Row 5 (RS) K1, [k9, k2tog, k9] over each of the 8 sections, k1—154 sts.
Rows 6–10 Work even in St st.
Row 11 K1, [k8, k2tog, k9] over each of the 8 sections, k1—146 sts.
Rows 12–16 Work even in St st.
Row 17 K1, [k8, k2tog, k8] over each of the 8 sections, k1—138 sts.

Rows 18–22 Work even in St st.
Row 23 K1, [k7, k2tog, k8] over each of the 8 sections, k1—130 sts.
Rows 24–28 Work even in St st.
Row 29 K1, [k7, k2tog, k7] over each of the 8 sections, k1—122 sts.
Rows 30–34 Work even in St st.
Row 35 K1, [k6, k2tog, k7] over each of the 8 sections, k1—114 sts.
Rows 36–40 Work even in St st.
Row 41 K1, [k6, k2tog, k6] over each of the 8 sections, k1—106 sts.
Rows 42–46 Work even in St st.
Row 47 K1, [k5, k2tog, k6] over each of the 8 sections, k1—98 sts.
Rows 48–42 Work even in St st.
Row 53 K1, [k5, k2tog, k5] over each of the 8 sections, k1—90 sts.
Rows 54–58 Work even in St st.
Row 59 K1, [k4, k2tog, k5] over each of the 8 sections, k1—82 sts.
Rows 60–64 Work even in St st.
Row 65 K1, [k4, k2tog, k4] over each of the 8 sections, k1—74 sts.
Rows 66–70 Work even in St st.
Row 71 K1, [k3, k2tog, k4] over each of the 8 sections, k1—66 sts; 8 sts in each section plus 2 edge sts.
Work 2 rows even in St st. Cut yarns and leave sts on spare needle, ready for a WS row.

LACE OVERLAY
With A and larger needles, cast on 197 sts.
Row 1 and all WS rows Purl.
Rows 2, 4, 6, 8, 10, and 12 K1, [yo, k3, SKP, yo, SK2P, yo, k2tog, k3, yo, k1] 14 times.
Row 14 (RS) [K3tog] 65 times, k2tog—66 sts.
Slip overlay to scrap yarn, pin for blocking, pinning out the points, and steam lightly.
Place WS of overlay on RS of skirt, ready for a WS row.

JOIN LAYERS
Row 15 (WS) Work 3-needle join purlwise over both pieces—66 sts.
Row 16 (RS) Cast on 2 sts, ([p1, k1] over these sts, p1) for ribbed band, k65—68 sts.
Row 17 Cast on 2 sts, ([k1, p1] over these sts, k1) for ribbed band, p to last 3 sts, rib to end—70 sts. Cut A.

BODICE
Row 1 (RS) With B, rib 3 sts, k29; k6 A; with B, k29, rib 3 sts.
Row 2 With B, rib 3 sts, p29; p6 A; with B, p29, rib 3 sts.
Rows 3–8 Rep last 2 rows 3 more times.

COLOR SHIFT #1
Row 9 With B, rib 3 sts, k28, k8 A, with B, k28, rib 3 sts.
Row 10 With B, rib 3 sts, p28, p8 A, with B, k28, rib 3 sts.
Rows 11–14 Rep last 2 rows twice more.

DIVIDE FOR BACKS AND FRONT
Row 15 (RS) With B, rib 3 sts, k14 for left back and sl these 17 sts to a holder; bind off 4 sts for left armhole; work until there are 10 B sts on needle, k8 A, k10 B and sl these 28 sts to holder for front; with B, bind off 4 sts for right armhole; work to end—17 sts for right back.

RIGHT BACK
SHAPE ARMHOLE
Row 16 With B, work even.
Row 17 (RS) K2tog, k12, rib 3 sts—16 sts.
Row 18 Work even.
Row 19 K2tog, k11, rib 3 sts—15 sts.
Rows 20–28 Work even.
Row 29 (RS) Bind off 6 sts for shoulder, work to end—9 sts. Place on holder for right back neck.

LEFT BACK
Sl 17 sts back to needle, ready for a WS row. Join B.
Row 16 (WS) With B, work even.

SHAPE ARMHOLE
Row 17 Rib 3 sts, k12, k2tog—16 sts.
Row 18 Work even.
Row 19 Rib 3 sts, k11, k2tog—15 sts.
Rows 20–28 Work even.
Row 29 K9 and place on holder for left back neck, bind off 6 sts for shoulder.

FRONT
Sl 28 sts back to needle, ready for a WS row, and join B.
Row 16 P10 B, p8 A, join second ball of B and p10.

SHAPE ARMHOLE AND COLOR SHIFT #2
Row 17 (dec) With B, ssk, k7; k10 A; with B, k7, k2tog—26 sts.
Row 18 Work even.
Row 19 (dec) With B, ssk, k6; k10 A; with B, k6, k2tog—24 sts.
Rows 20–22 Work even.

DIVIDE NECK
Row 23 K7 B, k2 A for left side and place on holder; k6 A and place on second holder for neck; k2 A, k7 B for right side—9 sts each side of neck.

RIGHT SIDE NECK SHAPING
Work on 9 sts for right side of neck as foll:
Row 24 P7 B, p2 A.

COLOR SHIFT #3
Row 25 (RS) K3 A, k6 B—9 sts.
Row 26 P6 B, p3 A.
Row 27 (dec) With A, ssk, k1, k6 B—8 sts.
Row 28 P6 B, k2 A.
Row 29 (dec) With A, ssk, k6 B—7 sts. Bind off.

LEFT SIDE COLOR SHIFT AND NECK SHAPING
Slip 9 sts to needle, ready for a WS row. Rejoin yarns.
Row 24 P2 A, p7 B.

COLOR SHIFT #3
Row 25 (RS) K6 B, k3 A—9 sts.
Row 26 P3 A, p6 B.
Row 27 (dec) K6 B, with A, k1, ssk—8 sts.
Row 28 P2A, p6 B.
Row 29 (dec) K6 B, with A ssk—7 sts. Bind off.

SLEEVE
With larger needles and A, cast on 22 sts. Knit 3 rows. Cut A.
With C, beg with a knit row, work 4 rows in St st.
Inc row (RS) K1, CO1, knit to last st, CO1, k1—24 sts.
Cont in St st, rep inc row every 6th row 2 more times—28 sts.
Work in St st until sleeve measures 3"/7.5cm above A, end with a RS row.

SHAPE CAP
Bind off 2 sts at beg of next 2 rows—24 sts.
Row 1 (RS) Ssk, knit to last 2 sts, k2tog—22 sts.
Row 2 Purl.
Rows 3 and 4 Rep rows 1 and 2—20 sts.

Row 5 Knit.
Row 6 Purl.
Rows 7–12 Rep rows 1 and 2 three times—14 sts.
Row 13 K1, [k3tog] 4 times, k1—6 sts.
Row 14 [P2tog] twice, pass first st over 2nd st, p2tog, pass first st over 2nd st and fasten off.

FINISHING
Sew shoulder seams.

NECKBAND
With larger needles, RS facing and A, pick up and k 3 sts across left back ribbing, k7 from left back holder, pick up and k 8 sts along left front, edge, k6 from front neck holder, pick up and k 8 sts along right front, k7 from right back holder, pick up and k 3 sts along right back rib—40 sts. Knit 3 rows. Bind off. Sew sleeve seams and sew into armholes.

Sew back skirt seam from cast-on row to joining row. Sew 3 snaps evenly to back of bodice. Using photo as a guide, criss-cross ribbon over color A section of bodice, sew in place. Sew small cameo or jewel to center front of neckband. Thread ribbon through row 14 of overlay, tie a bow at the back.

CROWN
With smaller needles and scrap yarn, cast on 51 sts using provisional cast-on method. Change to D.

PICOT HEM
Rows 1–3 Work in St st.
Row 4 (picot) (WS) P1, [yo, p2tog] 25 times.
Rows 5–7 Work in St st.

CROWN TOP
Carefully remove scrap yarn and place cast-on sts on a spare needle, ready for a WS row.
Row 8 Fold hem to WS at picot row, hold both needles parallel and work 3-needle join purlwise until all sts are joined.
Row 9 K1, (k2, yo, ssk, yo, [k1tbl, p1] twice, SK2P, [p1, k1tbl] twice, yo) 3 times, k2tog, yo, k3.
Row 10 P1, p2tog, yo, p2, (p1tbl, yo, p1tbl, k1, p1tbl, SP2P, p1tbl, k1, p1tbl, yo, p1tbl,p2, yo, ssp) 3 times, p1.

Row 11 K1, (k2, yo, ssk, k1tbl, p1, yo, k1tbl, p1, SK2P, p1, k1tbl, yo, p1, k1tbl) 3 times, k2tog, yo, k3.
Row 12 P1, p2tog, yo, p2, (p1tbl, k1, p1tbl, yo, p1tbl, SP2P, p1tbl, yo, p1tbl, k1, p1tbl, p2, yo, ssp) 3 times, p1.
Row 13 K1, (k2, yo, ssk, [k1tbl, p1] twice, yo, SK2P, yo, [p1, k1tbl] twice) 3 times, k2tog, yo, k3.
Row 14 P1, p2tog, yo, p2, (yo, [p1tbl, k1] twice, SP2P, [k1, p1tbl] twice, yo, p2, yo, ssp) 3 times, p1.
Row 15 K1, (k2, yo, ssk, k1tbl, yo, k1tbl, p1, k1tbl, SK2P, k1tbl, p1, k1tbl, yo, k1tbl) 3 times, k2tog, yo, k3.
Row 16 P1, p2tog, yo, p2, (p1tbl, k1, yo, p1tbl, k1, SP2P, k1, p1tbl, yo, k1, p1tbl, p2, yo, ssp) 3 times, p1.

Row 17 K1, (k2, yo, ssk, k1tbl, p1, k1tbl, yo, k1tbl, SK2P, k1tbl, yo, k1tbl, p1, k1tbl) 3 times, k2tog, yo, k3.
Row 18 P1, p2tog, yo, p2, ([p1tbl, k1] twice, yo, SP2P, yo, [k1, p1tbl] twice, p2, yo, ssp) 3 times, p1.
Row 19 (RS) Cast on 20 sts, [k1, p1] over these sts, [k1, p1] to end.
Row 20 Cast on 20 sts, [p1, k1] over these sts, [p1, k1] to end—91 sts.
Rows 21–2 K the knit sts, p the purl sts. Bind off.

Sew snap to ends. If desired, run elastic thread through band to fit your doll. Sew 3 jewels to front of crown, one under each point. Insert craft wire behind picot edge to support top of crown. See photo. ✳

49

Gnome Girl

*"So Many Gardens Have a Gnome
They Make Themselves Feel Right at Home"*

●●●○

MATERIALS

- 1 package of eight .35oz/10g skeins (each approx 28yd/26m) of Lion Brand *Bonbons* (cotton) in #630 beach: yellow (A), turquoise (B), seafoam green (C), purple (D), black (E), orange (F), red (G), and white (H) (**2**)
- One pair size 3 (3.25mm) needles OR SIZE TO OBTAIN GAUGE
- Size 3 (3.25mm) circular needle, 16"/40cm long
- One set (5) size 3 (3.25mm) double-pointed needles (dpns)
- 3 small round gold shank buttons
- 4 snaps
- Sewing needle and thread
- One 1¼"/3cm buckle
- 11"/28cm of ¼"/.5cm-width elastic
- 2 removable stitch markers
- 2 stitch holders
- 2 small jingle bells
- Two 6"/15.5cm lengths of leather cord or ribbon

GAUGE

24 sts and 34 rows to 4"/10cm over St st using size 3 (3.25mm) needles. TAKE TIME TO CHECK GAUGE.

K1, P1 RIB

(over an even number of sts)
Row 1 (RS) *K1, p1; rep from * to end.
Row 2 K the knit sts and p the purl sts.
Rep row 2 for k1, p1 rib.

TUNIC

FRONT
With A and straight needles, cast on 46 sts. Work in St st (knit on RS, purl

on WS) for 5 rows, end with a RS row. Knit 1 row on WS for turning ridge. Change to B.
Cont in St st, dec 1 st each side every 6th row 6 times—34 sts, place st markers on last set of decreases. Work even until piece measures 5"/12.5cm from turning ridge, end with a WS row.

SHAPE SLEEVES

Cast on 17 sts at beg of next 2 rows for sleeves—68 sts. Work even until sleeves measure 2"/5cm, end with a WS row.

SHAPE NECK

Next row (RS) K28 for left back, join

2nd ball of B, bind off 12 sts, k to end for right back—28 sts each side of neck. Working both sides of back at once with separate balls of yarn, work 2 rows even.

BACK

Change to C, work 2 more rows on both sides of back.
Next row (WS) On right side of back, p28; on left side of back, cast on 10 sts and, working over these sts, [p1, k1] twice, purl to end—38 sts.
Next row On left side of back, knit to last 4 sts, work in k1, p1 rib over last 4 sts; on right side of back, cast on 10 sts and, working over these sts, [k1, p1] twice, knit to end—38 sts.

Work even over both sides of back in St st with 4 rib sts as established until 2"/5cm from color change, end with a WS row.
Bind off 17 sleeve sts at beg of next 2 rows—21 sts each side.
Work until back measures same length as front to decrease markers when folded at color change. Cont in pats, inc 1 st each side every 6th row 6 times—27 sts each side.
Work even until backs measure same as front to 1 row less than turning ridge, end with a WS row. Change to A and St st over all sts. Knit 1 row on RS, then knit 1 row on WS for turning ridge. Cont in St st only for hem for 5 rows. Bind off.

POCKETS

(make 2)
With D, cast on 12 sts.
Work in St st for 1½"/4cm, end

sts. Beg with a RS row, knit 4 rows. Work in St st, inc 1 st each side every 4th row 4 times—40 sts. Work even until piece measures 4"/10cm from beg, end with a WS row.

SHAPE CROTCH
Bind off 3 sts at beg of next 2 rows, then 1 st at beg of next 2 rows—32 sts. Work even for 1"/2.5cm. Change to E and cont in St st for 1½"/4cm more, end with a RS row. Knit 1 row on WS for turning ridge. Work in St st until ½"/1.5cm above turning ridge for waistband. Bind off.

FINISHING
Sew crotch, front, back, and leg seams. Fold waistband to WS along turning ridge and sew in place, leaving small opening for elastic. Feed elastic through opening, into and around waistband to other side, secure elastic with sewing thread, and sew opening closed.

VEST
Note Vest is worked in one piece. With F, cast on 54 sts. Knit 1 row, purl 1 row.

SHAPE FRONTS
Cont in St st, inc 1 st each side every other row 5 times—64 sts. Work even until piece measures 1 ¾"/4.5cm from beg, end with a WS row.

DIVIDE FOR FRONTS AND BACK
Next row (RS) K13 for right front and sl to holder, bind off 4 sts for right armhole, knit until there are 30 sts on RH needle and sl to holder for back, bind off 4 sts for left armhole, knit to end—13 sts for left front.

LEFT FRONT
Work even in St st on 13 sts for left front until armhole measures ¾"/2cm, end with a RS row.

SHAPE NECK
Bind off 1 st at neck edge (beg WS rows) every other row 4 times—9 sts. Work even in St st until armhole measures 2"/5cm. Bind off.

with a RS row. Knit 1 row on WS. Bind off.
Embroider flower to center of each pocket as foll: With A, make 3 French knots for center of flower. With H, using lazy daisy st, make 5 petals around the center knots.
Sew pockets to front, using photo as guide.

FINISHING
Sew side and sleeve seams. Fold hem to WS along turning ridge and sew in place.

NECK TRIM
With RS facing, circular needle and A, pick up and k 46 sts along neck edge for neck trim. Do *not* join. Beg with a purl row on WS, work back and forth in St st for 5 rows. Bind off knitwise on RS. Trim will roll to RS with purl side showing.

With sewing needle and thread, sew 3 snaps to ribbed back bands with 1 snap 4"/10cm up from turning ridge, 1 snap just below neck trim, and one snap evenly spaced between. Sew 3 buttons along center front (see photo for placement).

PANTS
LEGS (make 2)
With straight needles and D, cast on 32

RIGHT FRONT

Place 13 right front sts on needle, ready for a WS row. Rejoin F.
Work even in St st until armhole measures ¾"/2cm, end with a WS row.

SHAPE NECK

Bind off 1 st at neck edge (beg RS rows) every other row 4 times—9 sts.
Work even in St st until armhole measures 2"/5cm. Bind off.

BACK

Place 30 back sts on needle, ready for a WS row. Rejoin F. Work even in St st until armhole measures 2"/5cm, end with a WS row.
Next row (RS) Bind off 9 sts for right back shoulder, knit until there are 12 sts on RH needle and sl to holder for back neck, bind off last 9 sts for left back shoulder.
Sew shoulder seams.

ARMHOLE TRIM

With RS facing, dpn and F, pick up and knit 36 sts evenly around right armhole. Join and place marker for beg of rnd.
Knit 3 rnds. Bind off.
Rep for left armhole.

VEST TRIM

With RS facing, circular needle and F, pick up and knit 114 sts along entire outer edge of vest, including 12 sts from back neck holder. Join and place marker for beg of rnd.
Knit 3 rnds. Bind off.
With H, embroider 5 X's along each front edge (see photo for placement).

BELT

With A, cast on 9 sts.
Work in k1, p1 rib for 11"/28cm. Bind off. Slide buckle to center of belt. Sew snap to ends.

HAT (make 2 pieces)

With G, cast on 40 sts. Knit 6 rows.

BEG SHAPING

Next (dec) row (RS) K1, k2tog, knit to last 3 sts, ssk, k1—2 sts dec'd.
Next row Purl.
Rep last 2 rows 17 more times—4 sts.
Next (dec) row (RS) Ssk, k2tog—2 sts.
Next (dec) row (WS) P2tog. Fasten off.

FINISHING

With RS tog, sew side edge seams. Turn RS out.

Embroider flower same as on pocket of tunic, at lower edge of hat (see photo).

BOOTS (make 2)

With G, cast on 46 sts.
Beg with a knit row, work in St st for 2 rows.
Dec row (RS) K1, ssk, k to last 3 sts, k2tog, k1—2 sts dec'd.
Purl 1 row.
Rep last 2 rows twice more—40 sts.
Dec row (RS) K1, [ssk] 3 times, k to last 7 sts, [k2tog] 3 times, k1—6 sts dec'd.
Purl 1 row.
Rep last 2 rows twice more—22 sts.
Work even in St st for 8 rows, ending with a WS row.
Picot row (RS) *K2tog, yo; rep from *, end k2tog—21 sts. Purl next row on WS, working p1 into each yo. Cont in St st for 4 more rows. Bind off. Fold hem to WS at picot row and sew in place.
With RS tog, fold boot in half. Beg at end of hem, sew side edges tog for front of boot, then seam along cast-on row for bottom of foot. Turn RS out. Shape point of boot and sew 1 jingle bell to each point. Tie leather cord around ankle of each boot. ✹

Forest Bride

*"The Enchanted Forest Bride Will Wear
A Gown Designed With Nature's Flair"*

MATERIALS

- 1 .88oz/25g ball (each approx 144yd/131m) of S. Charles Collezione *Crystal* (polyester/cotton) in #22 paper moon (A) (0)
- 2 .88oz/25g ball (each approx 232yd/212.5m) of S. Charles Collezione *Luna* (super kid mohair/silk/metallic) in #8 milky way (B) (0)
- 2 .88oz/25g ball (each approx 76.5yd/70m) of S. Charles Collezione *Stella* (silk/metallic) in #42 moonlight (C) (4)
- 1 .88oz/25g ball (each approx 132yd/120m) of Filatura di Crosa/Tahki•Stacy Charles *New Smoking* (viscose/polyester) in #2 silver (D) (2)
- One pair each sizes 5 and 7 (3.75 and 4.5mm) needles OR SIZE TO OBTAIN GAUGE
- Size F/5 (3.75mm) crochet hook
- Small pearl button for gown back
- 4 "diamond" beads or buttons for gown front
- 9 silver rosebuds for cape
- 6"/15cm of crystal beaded fringe for cape neck
- Approx 12 small white petal flowers with pearl centers for cape
- Half pearls in assorted sizes for cape
- 1yd/1m of 1½"/4cm sheer ribbon in silver-gray for headband
- 7 small silk roses in burgundy for headband
- 8"/20.5cm of 1½"/4cm silver

silk ribbon or fabric for belt
- 1 small snap for belt
- Stitch holders
- Glue
- Sewing needle and thread

GAUGES

- 18 sts and 28 rows to 4"/10cm over St st (knit on RS, purl on WS) using larger needles and 1 strand each of A and B held tog.
- 24 sts and 32 rows to 4"/10cm over St st using smaller needles and C.
TAKE TIME TO CHECK GAUGES.

NOTE
You can purchase a variety of embellishments at craft stores and combine them with the knitted flowers as shown here.

GOWN
BODY
With smaller needles and C, cast on 70 sts. Knit 2 rows. Cont in rev St st (purl on RS, knit on WS) until piece measures 10"/25.5cm from beg, end with a WS row.

DIVIDE FOR BODICE
Next row (RS) K16 for left back and place on holder, bind off 3 sts for left armhole, knit until there are 32 sts on RH needle for front and place on holder, bind off 3 sts for right armhole, knit to end for right back—16 sts. Cut C. Change to larger needles and 1 strand each of A & B held tog.

RIGHT BACK
Next row (WS) With 1 strand each of A & B held tog, [p2, k2] 4 times.
Cont to k the knit sts and p the purl sts for k2, p2 rib until armhole measures 2½"/6.5cm. Bind off.

LEFT BACK
Sl 16 sts to needle, ready for a WS row.
Next row (WS) With 1 strand each of A & B held tog, [k2, p2] 4 times.
Cont to k the knit sts and p the purl sts for k2, p2 rib until armhole measures 2½"/6.5cm. Bind off.

FRONT

Sl 32 sts to needle, ready for a RS row.
Next row (RS) With 2 strands of B held tog, [k2, p2] 3 times, k8, [p2, k2] 3 times. Cont to k the knit sts and p the purl sts for k2, p2 rib until armhole measures 2½"/6.5cm. Bind off.

FINISHING

Sew shoulder seams over 8 shoulder sts on each side.
Sew side edges of body tog for back seam from cast-on edge to 1"/2.5cm below bodice. With RS facing, crochet hook and C, work sc along each side of center back opening, making a ch-4 button loop on left back. Sew pearl button to right back opposite button loop. Using photo as guide, sew 4 "diamonds" to center of bodice front.

LARGE FLOWERS

(make 3 with 1 strand each of A and B held tog, make 3 with 1 strand each of B and D held tog, make 3 with 2 strands of D held tog)
With smaller needles and 2 strands of yarn held tog, cast on 16 sts. Knit 1 row. Make loops as foll: *insert needle in next st, wrap yarn around 2 fingers of left hand 3 times, then over needle again (4 loops on fingers), draw 4 loops through st, insert LH needle through front loops and k them tog through back loops; rep from * in each st. Fasten off. Sew side edges tog to form flower. Sew rosettes or jewels in center of each flower.

SMALL FLOWERS

(make 13 with A and B held tog)
With smaller needles and 2 strands of yarn held tog, cast on 12 sts.
Work same as for large flowers, *but* wrap yarn around 1 finger of left hand 3 times. Sew burgundy rosettes to centers of 7 small flowers, rosettes or jewels in centers of rem 6 flowers.

CAPE

Note Cape is worked from the neck down.
With smaller needles and C, cast on 40 sts.
Knit 4 rows. Change to larger needles

and 1 strand each of A and B held tog.
Next row (RS) K1, [kfb] 38 times, k1—78 sts.
Work in St st until piece measures 6"/15cm from beg, end with a WS row.

SHAPE FRONTS

Inc row (RS) K1, kfb, k to last 2 sts, kfb, k1—80 sts. Cont in St st and rep inc row every other row 3 more times, then every 4th row 4 times—94 sts. Work even until piece measures 12"/30.5cm from beg, end with a WS row.

SHAPE LOWER EDGE

Bind off 2 sts at beg of next 6 rows, 3 sts at beg of next 10 rows, then 4 sts at beg of next 6 rows—28 sts. Piece should measure 17"/43cm from beg.
Bind off.

LEFT FRONT BAND

With RS facing, smaller needles and C, pick up and k 70 sts evenly along left front edge. Knit 2 rows. Bind off purlwise.

RIGHT FRONT BAND
With RS facing, smaller needles and C, pick up and k 70 sts evenly along right front edge. Knit 2 rows. Bind off purlwise.

PICOT EDGING
With RS facing, smaller needles and D, pick up and knit 134 sts along bound-off edge, working between sts when necessary. Knit 3 rows.
Bind-off row (RS) Bind off 2 sts, *slip the st on RH needle to LH needle, cast on 3 sts, bind off 5 sts; rep from * until 1 st rem. Fasten off.

FINISHING
CAPE
Using photo as a guide, embellish cape as desired with 9 large flowers, 6 small flowers, beads, jewels and half pearls. Sew beaded fringe to RS of neck edge.

HEADBAND
Tie the silver-gray sheer ribbon to fit your doll's head and make a small bow, leaving 5–6"/12.5–15cm ties at each end. Sew 7 small flowers around crown of headband, leaving ties undecorated.

BELT
Cut silver ribbon or fabric to fit around your doll's chest plus ½"/1cm extra. Fold in half lengthwise and sew edges tog. Sew snap half to each end. ✳

Mystical, Magical Birds' Nests

MATERIALS
- 1 1¾oz/50g skein (each 64yd/58m) of Lion Brand *Fun Fur* (polyester) in #320-100 white OR 1 1¾oz/50g skein (each 27yd/25m) skein of Lion Brand *Romance* (nylon/polyester) in #325-100 silky white
- Assorted leftover white and silver yarns ⑤
- One pair size 10 (6mm) needles OR SIZE TO OBTAIN GAUGE
- Purchased bird and eggs
- White feathers
- Small amount of roving or Polyfill for bedding
- Assortment of pearl beads and pendants
- Yarn and sewing thread
- Glue

GAUGE
12 sts and 24 rows to 4"/10cm over garter st using size 10 (6mm) needles and 1 strand of each yarn held tog. TAKE TIME TO CHECK GAUGE.

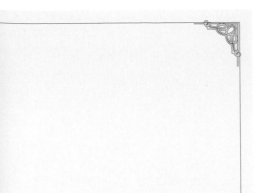

NOTE

Hold together leftover yarns in a variety of colors and textures to form these nests.

LARGE NEST

With 1 strand of each yarn held tog, cast on 36 sts.
Work in garter st (knit every row) for approx 3"/7.5cm.

BASE SHAPING

Row 1 (RS) [K7, k2tog] 4 times—32 sts.
Row 2 [K6, k2tog] 4 times—28 sts.
Row 3 [K5, k2tog] 4 times—24 sts.
Row 4 [K4, k2tog] 4 times—20 sts.
Row 5 [K3, k2tog] 4 times—16 sts.
Row 6 [K2, k2tog] 4 times—12 sts.
Row 7 [K1, k2tog] 4 times—8 sts.

FINISHING

Cut yarns, leaving a 6"/15cm tail. Draw tail through rem 8 sts, pull tog tightly, and secure the end. Sew side seam. Embellish with beads and feathers.

TINY NEST

With 2–3 thin yarns, cast on 20 sts. Knit 4 rows.

BASE SHAPING

Row 1 (RS) [K2tog] 10 times—10 sts.
Row 2 [K2tog] 5 times—5 sts.

FINISHING

Cut yarns, leaving a 4"/10cm tail. Draw tail through rem 5 sts, pull tog tightly, and secure the end. Sew side seam. ✳

NICKY'S WHIMSICAL RECIPE

Sparkle Egg Birds' Nests

MAKES 8 NESTS

INGREDIENTS

1 package (6oz/170g) chow mein noodles
1 package (12oz/340.2g) butterscotch or peanut butter–flavored candy wafers
1 package (2.8oz/80g) Jelly Belly sparkling jellybeans

1 cup flaked coconut
1 bottle of edible dust in silver or gold (optional)
Small soft paintbrush
Butter or butter spray
Cupcake tin
Microwaveable bowl

DIRECTIONS

1. Spray or butter cupcake pan and set aside.
2. Melt the candy wafers in a bowl in the microwave. Add chow mein noodles to bowl and gently coat with a spoon. Place approximately ⅓ cup of noodle mixture into each cupcake hole. Move the noodles from the center to the sides, making a crater in the center to look like a nest. Cool for 15 minutes in refrigerator.
3. Remove nests from cupcake tin by tapping the bottoms of each cup to loosen. Fill the nests with coconut and place jellybeans on top. If desired, brush the nests with edible dust.

Wonderful Wizard

●●○○

*"A Wizard's Wand Can Send a Beam
To Change a Frog into Ice Cream"*

MATERIALS
- 2 1¾oz/50g skeins (each approx 164yd/150m) of Premier *Spangle* (nylon/metallic) in #11-214 royalty (A) (3)
- 1 1¾oz/50g skein (each approx 34yd/31m) of Premier *Lash Lux Sequins* (polyester) in #8 Rio (B) (3)
- Small amount of Rowan *Anchor Artiste Metallic* (viscose, metalized polyester) in #300 gold (C) (3)
- One pair each sizes 4 and 6 (3.25 and 4mm) needles OR SIZE TO OBTAIN GAUGE
- Stitch markers
- Stitch holders
- 4 snaps
- 1 star-shaped shank button
- 1 manila file folder for hat stiffener
- Sewing needle and thread
- Fabric glue
- Embroidery needle

GAUGE
28 sts and 36 rows to 4"/10cm over St st (knit on RS, purl on WS) using smaller needles and A. TAKE TIME TO CHECK GAUGE.

NOTE
Robe is worked with A and trimmed with B. The stars and moon are embroidered with C in finishing.

BACK
With smaller needles and A, cast on 70 sts. Knit 3 rows.
Work in St st for 7 rows.

SHAPE SIDES
Next row (RS) K2tog, knit to last 2 sts, ssk—68 sts.
Cont in St st and rep dec row every 8th row 9 more times—50 sts.
Work even until piece measures 12"/30.5cm from beg. Bind off.

RIGHT FRONT
With smaller needles and A, cast on 35 sts. Knit 3 rows.
Work in St st for 7 rows.

SHAPE SIDE
Next row (RS) Knit to last 2 sts, ssk—34 sts.
Cont in St st and rep dec row every 8th

row 9 more times—25 sts.
Work even until piece measures 10"/25.5cm from beg, end with a WS row.

SHAPE NECK
Next row (RS) Bind off 5 sts, knit to end—20 sts.
Next row Purl.
Next row (RS) Bind off 1 st, knit to end—19 sts.
Work even until piece measures 12"/30.5cm from beg. Bind off.

LEFT FRONT
With smaller needles and A, cast on 35 sts. Knit 3 rows. Work in St st for 7 rows.

SHAPE SIDE
Next row (RS) K2tog, knit to end—34 sts. Cont in St st and rep dec row every 8th row 9 more times—25 sts. Work even until piece measures 10"/25.5cm from beg, end with a RS row.

SHAPE NECK
Next row (WS) Bind off 5 sts, purl to end—20 sts.
Next row Knit.
Next row (WS) Bind off 1 st, knit to end—19 sts.
Work even until piece measures 12"/30.5cm from beg. Bind off.

SLEEVES
With smaller needles and A, cast on 46 sts. Knit 3 rows.
Next row (RS) K2tog, knit to last 2 sts, ssk—44 sts.

Work in St st, and rep dec row every 4th row 3 more times—38 sts.
Work even until sleeve measures 2½"/6.5cm from beg. Bind off.

FINISHING
Sew shoulder seams. Place markers 2¼"/5.5cm down from shoulder on each side. Sew sleeves between markers. (Sleeve will gather slightly.) Sew side and sleeve seams.

FRONT BANDS
With RS facing, smaller needles and A, pick up and k 72 sts evenly along straight left front edge. Knit 6 rows. Bind off. Rep on right front edge

NECKBAND
With RS facing, smaller needles and A, beg at right front neck, pick up and k 45 sts evenly around neck edge. Knit 10 rows. Cut A, join C and knit 4 rows. Bind off. Sew first snap set to neckband. Sew rem 3 snap sets at 2"/5cm intervals along front bands. Sew button to neckband, using photo as guide.

FUR TRIM
LOWER EDGE
With larger needles and B, cast on 110 sts. Knit 2 rows. Bind off knitwise. Pin and sew to cast-on edge of robe.

SLEEVE EDGE (make 2)
With larger needles and B, cast on 36 sts. Complete same as lower edge trim.

EMBROIDERY
With embroidery needle and C, embroider stars in different sizes to fronts as desired. See diagram.

HAT (make 2 pieces)
With smaller needles and A, cast on 48 sts. Knit 3 rows. Purl 1 row.
Next row (RS) K1, ssk, k to last 3 sts, k2tog, k1—46 sts.
Cont in St st, rep dec row every RS row 21 more times—4 sts. Purl 1 row.
Next row (RS) K2tog twice—2 sts. P2tog. Fasten off. With embroidery needle and C, embroider stars in different sizes as desired. See diagram. Using duplicate st and C, embroider moon where desired, following chart.

FUR TRIM
With larger needles and B, cast on 72 sts. Knit 2 rows. Bind off knitwise. Pin and sew to lower edge of hat.

PAPER INSERT
Use template on page 117 to cut shape from manila folder. Wrap to form a cone and secure edges with tape. Brush cone lightly with glue. (A child's party hat can also be used.)

FINISHING
Sew the 2 knitted hat pieces tog. Starting at top point, carefully place knit hat over the cone. Press fur at edge firmly. ✳

MOON CHART   STAR DIAGRAM

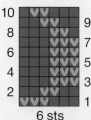

STITCH KEY

Ⅴ   duplicate st in C

| straight st in C

63

Golden Princess

*"She Was a Sight to Behold
When Midas Turned Her Into Gold"*

●●●○

MATERIALS
- 1 1¾oz/50g skein (each approx 202yd/185m) of Lion Brand *Vanna's Glamour* (acrylic/metallic polyester) in #171 gold (**2**)
- One pair each sizes 3 and 8 (3.25 and 5mm) needles OR SIZE TO OBTAIN GAUGE
- Two size 3 (3.25mm) double-pointed needles (dpns)
- Stitch holders
- Four ¼" (6mm) pearl buttons in gold
- 13"/33cm of 1"/2.5cm-wide gold ribbon for belt
- 1yd/1m beaded fringe
- 3 small ribbon rosettes in gold
- One ¾"(19mm) topaz bead for crown
- 12 x 12"/30.5 x 30.5cm of gold tulle for crown veil

GAUGE
20 sts and 24 rows to 4"/10cm over St st (knit on RS, purl on WS) using larger needles. TAKE TIME TO CHECK GAUGE.

RUCHING PATTERN
(over any number of sts)
Row 1 (RS) With larger needles, kfb in each st across—stitch count is doubled.
Rows 2, 4, 6, and 8 (WS) Purl.
Rows 3, 5, and 7 Knit.
Row 9 With smaller needles, k2tog across—stitch count is halved.
Rows 10–12 Knit.
Rep rows 1–12 for ruching pat.

I-CORD
With dpns, cast on 5 sts. *Knit 1 row. Without turning work, slide the sts back to the opposite end of needle to work next row from RS. Pull yarn tightly from the end of the row. Rep from * for desired length. Bind off.

NOTE
Skirt is worked from side to side, with the cast-on and bound-off edges sewn tog in finishing for the back seam. The bodice sts are picked up and knit along one side edge of the skirt.

GOWN
SKIRT
With smaller needles, cast on 40 sts. Work rows 1–12 of ruching pat 13 times, then rep rows 1–10 once more. Bind off loosely, knitwise.

BODICE
Row 1 (RS) With larger needles and RS facing, cast on 2 sts, work along one side edge of skirt and pick up and k 4 sts in rows 2–8 of each of the 14 ruching pat reps, cast on 2 sts—60 sts.
Rows 2–4 Knit.
Row 5 K1, p1, knit to last 2 sts, p1, k1.
Row 6 P1, k1, purl to last 2 sts, k1, p1.
Rows 7–12 Rep rows 5 and 6 three more times.

DIVIDE FOR FRONT AND BACKS
Next row (RS) K1, p1, k12, k2tog and place these 15 sts on a st holder for left back; k2tog, k24, k2tog and place these 26 sts on a st holder for front; k2tog, k12, p1, k1 for right back—15 sts.

RIGHT BACK
Work even on 15 sts for 1½"/4cm, end with a RS row.

NECK SHAPING
Row 1 (WS) Bind off 2 sts, purl to last 6 sts, and place 7 sts just worked on a holder for right back, p6.
Row 2 K6.
Rows 3 and 4 Work even in St st.
Row 5 P2tog, p4—5 sts.
Row 6 K3, k2tog—4 sts.
Bind off.

LEFT BACK
Sl 15 sts to larger needle, ready for a WS row. Join yarn and work even for 1½"/4cm, end with a WS row.

NECK SHAPING
Row 1 (RS) Bind off 2 sts, knit to last 6 sts, place 7 sts just worked on a holder for left back neck, k6.
Row 2 P6.
Rows 3 and 4 Work even in St st.
Row 5 K2tog, k4—5 sts.
Row 6 P3, p2tog—4 sts. Bind off.

FRONT
Sl 26 sts to larger needle, ready for a WS row. Join yarn and work in St st for 1½"/4cm, end with a WS row.

NECK SHAPING
LEFT SIDE
Row 1 (RS) K6 for left side of neck, place next 20 sts on st holder.
Work on 6 sts as foll:
Rows 2–4 Work even in St st.
Row 5 K4, k2tog—5 sts.
Row 6 P2tog, p3—4 sts. Bind off.
Keep center 14 sts on holder, sl last 6 sts to larger needle for right side of neck, ready for a RS row.

RIGHT SIDE
Work on 6 sts as foll:
Rows 1– 4 Work even in St st.
Row 5 (RS) K2tog, k4—5 sts.
Row 6 P3, p2tog—4 sts. Bind off.

SLEEVES
With smaller needles, cast on 20 sts.
Change to larger needles. Work rows
1–12 of ruching pat once. Cont in St st
with larger needles for 4"/10cm above
ruching pat.
Knit 3 rows. Bind off knitwise.

FINISHING
NECKBAND
Sew shoulder seams. With RS facing and
larger needles, k7 from left back holder,
pick up and k 11 sts along left
neck/shoulder edge, k14 from front
holder, pick up and k 11 sts along right
neck/shoulder edge, k7 from right back
holder—50 sts.
Knit 3 rows. Bind off knitwise.

Sew sleeve seams. Sew cast-on edge of
sleeves to armholes.
Sew cast-on edge of skirt to bound-off
edge for back seam.
Sew 4 small buttons evenly spaced to
RS of right back opening. Poke the
buttons through sts in purl column of
left back opening.
Sew rosettes to front neck, using photo
as guide.

CROWN
Make three I-cords, each approx
19"/48cm long. Sew the 3 cast-on ends
tog, braid the cords, sew bound-off ends
tog. Sew beaded fringe to edge of braid
along WS. Sew ends of braid tog to form
approx 15"/38cm crown. Sew jewel to
front of crown, using photo as guide.
Cut 8"/20cm circle of tulle, sew circle
center to back of crown on WS for veil.

BELT
Cut lengths of ribbon and beaded fringe to
fit around doll's waist. Sew beaded fringe
to hang from one edge of ribbon, fold
ribbon in half lengthwise so that fringe is
on WS. Sew ribbon edges tog lengthwise.
Sew snaps to end of ribbon. ✳

Mystical Mermaid

*"The Mermaid Lives Beneath the Sea
And Hopes a Sailor Comes to Tea"*

MATERIALS
- 1 1¾oz/50g ball (each approx 204yd/187m) of Crystal Palace Yarns *Panda Silk* (bamboo/superwash merino wool/silk) each in #5140 blue lagoon (A), #3024 aquarium (B), and #3036 ocean (C) ▪
- Small amount of gold metallic DK-weight yarn for flowers (D) ▪
- Small amount of DK-weight yarn in orange, or desired color, for starfish ▪
- One pair size 1 (2.25mm) needles OR SIZE TO OBTAIN GAUGE
- One pair each sizes 2 and 8 (2.75 and 5mm) needles
- Six size 2 (2.75mm) double-pointed needles (dpns) for starfish
- Two size 5 (3.75mm) dpns for headband
- Size D/3 (3.25mm) crochet hook
- Small stitch holders
- 4 removable stitch markers
- 4 snaps
- Blue ribbon to coordinate with yarn colors: ⅜"/10mm wide and 30"/76cm long
- Yarn needle
- 25 small white pearls for starfish
- Assorted small beads, pearls, shells, and charms with holes for sewing
- Sewing needle and thread

GAUGES
- 32 sts and 40 rows to 4"/10cm over St st using size 1 (2.25mm) needles and B.
- 24 sts and 32 rows to 4"/10cm over scales pat using size 1 (2.25mm) needles and A.

TAKE TIME TO CHECK GAUGES.

STITCH GLOSSARY
kfb Knit into front and back of 1 st to inc 1 st.

pfkb Purl into front and knit into back of 1 st to inc 1 st.

CO1 (cast on 1—inc) Wrap yarn around left thumb from back to front. Insert RH needle from front into the loop on thumb. Remove thumb from loop and tighten loop on needle (also called wrap cast-on). 1 stitch has been increased.

DRESS
SKIRT
With A and size 1 (2.25mm) needles, cast on 82 sts.

BEGIN SCALES PATTERN
Row 1 (WS) K1, [k1, yo, p6, yo, k1] 10 times, k1—102 sts.

Row 2 (RS) K1, [p1, yo, k8, yo, p1] 10 times, k1—122 sts.

Row 3 K1, [k1, yo, k10, yo, k1] 10 times, k1—142 sts.

Row 4 K1, purl to last st, k1.

Row 5 K1, *k1, [insert needle knitwise into next st and (yo) 3 times, draw these 3 loops through st] 12 times, k1; rep from * for a total of 10 reps, k1.

Row 6 K1, *p1, [(slip next st purlwise and drop 2 of the 3 wraps) twice, sl last 2 sts back to LH needle and k2tog] 6 times, p1; rep from * for a total of 10 reps, k1—82 sts. Rep rows 1–6 a total of 13 times, rep row 1 once more—102 sts.

HIPS
Row 2 (RS) K21, [place marker (pm), work row 2 of scales pat as established over next 20 sts, pm, k20] twice, k1—110 sts.

Row 3 (WS) K1, p20, [slip marker (sm), work row 3 of scales pat as established to next marker, sm, p20] twice, k1—118 sts.

Row 4 K1, CO1, k20, [sm, work row 4 of scales pat to next marker, sm, k20] twice, CO1, k1—122 sts.

Row 5 P22, [sm, work row 5 of scales pat to next marker, sm, p20] twice, p2.

Row 6 K22, [sm, work row 6 of scales pat to next marker, sm, k20] twice, k2—96 sts.

Row 7 Purl, removing markers, cut A.

BODICE
Join B and work in St st (knit on RS, purl on WS) for 2½"/6.5cm, end with a WS row.

DIVIDE FOR FRONT AND BACKS
Next row (RS) K20 for left back and slip to stitch holder, bind off 12 sts for left armhole, knit until there are 32 sts for front and sl to stitch holder, bind off 12 sts for right armhole, knit to end—20 sts for right back.

RIGHT BACK
Beg with a WS row, work 8 rows even in St st.

FRONT
Row 1 (WS) P20, cast on 4 sts, pm, p 32 front sts from holder—56 sts.

Row 2 (RS) K 32 front sts.

Row 3 P 32 front sts.

Row 4 K 32 front sts, k 1 cast-on st for shoulder. Turn.
Row 5 P33.
Row 6 K 32 front sts, k 1 shoulder st, k 1 cast-on st. Turn.
Row 7 P34.
Row 8 K 32 front sts, k 2 shoulder sts, k 1 cast-on st. Turn.
Row 9 P35.
Row 10 K 32 front sts, k 3 shoulder sts, k 1 cast-on st. Turn.

LEFT BACK

Row 11 (WS) P36, cast on 4 sts, pm, p 20 left back sts from holder—80 sts on needle. Cont to work on left back sts only as foll:
Row 12 (RS) K 20 left back sts.
Row 13 P 20 left back sts.
Row 14 K 20 left back sts, k1 cast-on st for shoulder. Turn.
Row 15 P21.
Row 16 K 20 left back sts, k 1 shoulder st, k1 cast-on st. Turn.
Row 17 P22 sts.
Row 18 K 20 left back sts, k 2 shoulder sts, k 1 cast-on st. Turn.
Row 19 P 23 left back sts.

JOIN FOR YOKE

Row 20 K 20 left back sts, k 3 shoulder sts, k 1 cast-on st, k to end—80 sts. Cont on all 80 sts as foll:
Row 21 Purl.
Row 22 [K to marker, sm, k2tog] twice, k to end—78 sts.
Row 23 [P to 2 sts before marker, p2tog, sm] twice, p to end—76 sts.
Row 24 [K to 1 st before marker, remove marker, k2tog] twice, k to end—74 sts.
Row 25 Purl.
Row 26 Knit.
Rows 27–30 Purl.
Bind off purlwise.

FINISHING

Sew side edges tog from cast-on row to ½"/1.5cm above beg of hips for back seam. With crochet hook and B, work 1 row of sl st around back opening. Sew 4 snaps along back opening. With crochet hook and A, work a rnd of sl st around lower edge of dress, skipping every few sts to taper for mermaid tail. Using photo as inspiration, sew pearls and small beads to skirt front.

SEASHELL TOPS

SHELL (MAKE 2)
With C and size 1 (2.25mm) needles, cast on 41 sts.

BEGIN SHORT ROWS
Row 1 (RS) K1, [p3, k1] 10 times.
Row 2 (WS) P1, [k3, p1] 8 times, k3—5 sts rem at end of row. Turn.
Row 3 [P3, k1] 7 times, p3—5 sts rem at end of row. Turn.
Row 4 [K3, p1] 6 times, k3—9 sts rem at end of row. Turn.
Row 5 [P3, k1] 5 times, p3—9 sts rem at end of row. Turn.
Row 6 [K3, p1] 4 times, k3—13 sts rem at end of row. Turn.
Row 7 [P3, k1] 3 times, p3—13 sts rem at end of row. Turn.
Row 8 [K3, p1] 7 times. Turn. End of short rows.
Row 9 (RS) [K1, p2tog, p1] 10 times, k1—31 sts.
Row 10 [P1, k2tog] 10 times, p1—21 sts.
Row 11 Bind off 4 sts, work as established in rib to end—17 sts.
Row 12 Bind off 4 sts, [k2tog] 6 times—7 sts.
Row 13 Purl.
Row 14 K1, [k2tog] 3 times—4 sts.
Slip sts to holder, cut yarn.

JOIN SHELLS

Slip sts to size 1 (2.25mm) needle, ready for a RS row—8 sts.
Joining row (RS) With C, *pick up and k 2 sts in side edge of short rows (below bind-off row), k4 from needle, pick up and k 2 sts in side edge of short rows (below bind-off row); rep from * once—16 sts.
Knit 3 rows. Bind off.

FINISHING

Sew ribbon to WS of seashell top. Using photo as guide for placement, join C to cast-on row of left shell with crochet hook and ch for 3½"/9cm. Fasten off, join end to ribbon at 4½"/11.5cm from center of joining row. Rep for right shell.

Using photo as inspiration, embellish with pearls, shells, and beads as desired.

FLIPPERS

Make 4 pieces as foll:
With size 2 (2.75mm) needles and B, cast on 24 sts.

BEGIN SHORT ROWS
Row 1 (WS) K24.
Row 2 (RS) K24.
Row 3 K18—6 sts rem unworked. Turn.
Row 4 K18.
Row 5 K24.
Row 6 K24.
Row 7 Bind off 3 sts, purl to end.
Row 8 K21.
Row 9 K15—6 sts rem unworked. Turn.
Row 10 K15.
Rows 11–14 K21.
Row 15 Bind off 3 sts, purl to end.
Row 16 K18.
Row 17 K12—6 sts rem unworked. Turn.
Row 18 K12.
Row 19 K18.
Row 20 K18.
Row 21 K12—6 sts rem unworked. Turn.
Row 22 K12.
Row 23 P18.
Row 24 K18.
Row 25 K12—6 sts rem unworked. Turn.
Row 26 K12.
Row 27 K18.
Row 28 K18.
Row 29 K12—6 sts rem unworked. Turn.
Row 30 K12.
Row 31 Cast on 3 sts, p21.
Row 32 K21.
Row 33 K15—6 sts rem unworked. Turn.
Row 34 K15.
Row 35 K21.
Row 36 K21.
Row 37 K15—6 sts rem unworked. Turn.
Row 38 K15.
Row 39 Cast on 3 sts, p24.
Row 40 K24.
Row 41 K18—6 sts rem unworked. Turn.
Row 42 K18.
Rows 43–45 K24.
Bind off knitwise.
Set aside 2 pieces for flipper tops, work on 2 rem pieces as foll:

FLIPPER HEEL

With 2 (2.75mm) needles and B and RS of 1 flipper facing, pick up and k 14 sts along LH edge (end of RS rows).

Purl 1 row, knit 1 row, purl 1 row.
Row 1 (RS) Ssk, knit to last 2 sts, k2tog—12 sts.
Row 2 Purl.
Rows 3 and 4 Rep rows 1 and 2—10 sts.
Row 5 CO1, knit to end, CO1—12 sts.
Row 6 Purl.
Rows 7 and 8 Rep rows 5 and 6—14 sts.
Knit 1 row, purl 2 rows. Bind off.
Fold RS of heel tog at row 4, sew shaped side edges tog. Turn heel RS out.
Rep on 1 more flipper—2 flipper bottoms complete.
Place 1 flipper bottom and 1 flipper top tog with WS tog, matching shaped edge. With C and crochet hook, work 1 row of sl st around cast-on/bound-off edges and shaped edge, leaving foot opening plain.

Using photo as inspiration, embellish with pearls, shells, and beads as desired.

I-CORD HEADBAND
With 1 strand each of B, C, and D held tog, cast on 5 sts to one size 5 (3.75mm) dpn.
Knit 5, *sl sts back to opposite end of needle, k5; rep from * for I-cord until piece measures 16"/40.5cm. Bind off.

FINISHING
Form headband by making a circle of the I-cord and overlapping the ends by 1"/2.5cm. Using photo as guide, wrap the overlapped ends around I-cord and sew in place. Using photo as inspiration, sew 3 flowers to headband and embellish with pearls, shells, and beads as desired.

BUTTERCUP FLOWERS (MAKE 3)
With D and size 2 (2.75mm) needles, cast on 43 sts.
Row 1 (RS) *K1, yo, k5, (slip second, third, fourth, and fifth sts over first st), yo; rep from * to last st, k1—29 sts.
Row 2 P1, *p3tog, p1; rep from * to end—15 sts.
Row 3 K1, *k2tog; rep from * to end—8 sts.
Row 4 Pass the second, third, fourth, fifth, sixth, seventh, and eighth sts over the first st. Fasten off last st.
Sew side edges tog to form flower. Using photo as inspiration, embellish with pearls, shells, and beads as desired.

SHAWL
With C and size 8 (5mm) needles, cast on 24 sts.
Knit 4 rows.
Row 1 (RS) Sl 1, *k2tog, yo; rep from * to last st, k1.
Row 2 Sl 1, knit to end.
Rep last 2 rows until piece measures 28"/71cm from beg, end with a row 2.
Knit 4 rows. Bind off.
Note Shawl will bias; block to shape a rectangle.

STARFISH
With E, cast on 5 sts onto one size 2 (2.75mm) dpn.

Next row (RS) Kfb in each st—10 sts.
Sl 2 sts to each of 5 dpns.
Join to work in the rnd, being careful not to twist sts. Place removable marker on first st.
Work over EACH dpn as foll:
Rnd 1 [P1, kfb]—3 sts on each dpn.
Rnd 2 [K1, p1, kfb]—4 sts on each dpn.
Rnd 3 [P1, k1] twice.
Rnd 4 [Kfb, p1, k1, pfkb]—6 sts on each dpn.

SEPARATE FOR LEGS
*Work back and forth in rows over the next 6 sts as foll, leave the rem dpns to be worked later:
Row 1 (RS) K1, p1, k3, pfkb—7 sts.
Row 2 K1, [p1, k1] 3 times.
Row 3 K1, p1, k3, p1, k1.
Rows 4–9 Rep last 2 rows 3 more times.
Row 10 P2tog, k1, [p1, k1] twice—6 sts.
Row 11 P2tog, k3, p1—5 sts.
Row 12 P1, [k1, p1] twice.
Row 13 P1, k3, p1.
Row 14 K2tog, p1, k1, p1—4 sts.
Row 15 K2tog, k2—3 sts.
Bind off all sts.
Join yarn to next dpn, ready for RS row, and work from * for next leg until 5 legs are completed.

FINISHING
Sew 5 beads to center of each starfish leg, using photo as guide. Using photo as inspiration, sew starfish to shawl and decorate shawl with shells, beads, pearls, and charms. ✳

Whimsical Witch

●●●○

"Be Careful What You Say or Do:
This Witch Will Cast a Spell on You"

MATERIALS

- 2 1¾oz/50g skeins (each approx 166yd/152m) of Patons *Kroy Socks* (wool/nylon) in #55040 coal (A) (1)
- 1 skein in #55315 sweet stripes (B)
- One pair each sizes 4 and 6 (3.5 and 4mm) needles OR SIZE TO OBTAIN GAUGE
- Size E/4 (3.5mm) crochet hook
- 3 black snaps
- 2 removable stitch markers
- 2 stitch holders
- Sewing needle and black thread
- 8"/20.5cm length of ⅛"/3mm satin ribbon: black for collar; light blue for shoes
- Yarn needle for duplicate stitch
- Decorative pin for dress; spider web and spider pins for hat (optional)
- ¾"/2cm ribbon for belt; small piece of cardboard for buckle

NOTES

1) Almost all of A was used: if your gauge doesn't match, get an extra skein of yarn.
2) Cat and zigzag motifs are embroidered in duplicate stitch after dress is knit.

GAUGE

24 sts and 32 rows to 4"/10cm over St st using smaller needles. TAKE TIME TO CHECK GAUGE.

DRESS

SKIRT

With smaller needles and A, cast on 120 sts. Work in St st (knit on RS, purl on WS) for 4 rows. Purl 1 row on RS for turning ridge.

Work 3 more rows in St st, ending with a WS row.

BEGIN STRIPE PATTERN

Cont in St st, [work 2 rows B, 4 rows A] 4 times, work 10 rows B, 4 rows A, [work 2 rows B, 4 rows A] 4 times, work 10 rows B, work 2 rows A. Cont even with A only.

BODICE

Dec row (RS) *K2tog; rep from * to end—60 sts.
Work even in St st for 2"/5cm, end with a WS row.

DIVIDE FOR FRONT AND BACK

Next row (RS) K15 for left back and sl to holder, bind off 2 sts for left armhole, knit until there are 26 sts on RH needle

and sl to holder for front, bind off 2 sts for right armhole, knit to end—15 sts for right back.

RIGHT BACK

Next row (WS) Working on 15 sts for right back, purl.
Dec row (RS) K1, ssk, k to end—14 sts. Work even in St st until armhole measures 2½"/6.5cm, end with a WS row. Bind off.

LEFT BACK

Place 15 left back sts on smaller needle, ready for WS row. Rejoin A.
Next row (WS) Purl.
Dec row (RS) Knit to last 3 sts, k2tog, k1—14 sts.
Work even in St st until armhole measures 2½"/6.5cm, end with a WS row. Bind off.

FRONT

Place 26 front sts on smaller needle, ready for WS row. Rejoin A.
Next row (WS) Purl.
Dec row (RS) K1, ssk, knit to last 3 sts, k2tog, k1—24 sts. Work even in St st until armhole measures 2"/5cm, end with a WS row.

SHAPE NECK

Next row (RS) K9, join 2nd ball of A and bind off center 6 sts, knit to end—9 sts each side of neck.
Next row (WS) Purl across each side of neck.

Dec row (RS) Knit across left side of neck to last 2 sts, k2tog; on right side of neck, ssk, knit to end—8 sts rem each side for shoulder.

Work even in St st until armhole measures 2½"/6.5cm, end with a WS row. Bind off.

SLEEVES (make 2)

With smaller needles and A, cast on 23 sts. Work in St st for 3 rows. Knit 1 row on WS for turning ridge.

BEGIN STRIPE PATTERN

Cont in St st, [work 4 rows A, 2 rows B] 4 times, AT THE SAME TIME, inc 1 st each side every 4th row 4 times—31 sts. Work even in St st until sleeve measures 4"/10cm from turning ridge, end with a WS row.

SHAPE SLEEVE CAP

Bind off 2 sts at beg of next 4 rows— 23 sts.

Work even for 4 rows.

Dec 1 st each side every other row 4 times—15 sts.

Purl 1 row.

Dec row (RS) [Ssk] 3 times, SK2P, [k2tog] 3 times—7 sts.

Dec row (WS) P2tog, bind off to last 2 sts, p2tog, bind off rem st.

COLLAR

With smaller needles and B, cast on 5 sts.

Row 1 (RS) Sl 1, k1, [yo] twice, k2tog, k1—6 sts.

Row 2 Sl 1, k1, work (k1, p1) into double yo, k2.

Row 3 Sl 1, k3, [yo] twice, k2—8 sts.

Row 4 Sl 1, k1, work (k1, p1) into double yo, k4.

Row 5 Sl 1, k1, [yo] twice, k2tog, k4—9 sts.

Row 6 Sl 1, k4, work (k1, p1) into double yo, k2.

Row 7 Sl 1, k8.

Row 8 Bind off 4 sts, k to end—5 sts.

Rep rows 1–8 nine more times—10 points. Bind off rem sts.

FINISHING

CAT MOTIF

With RS facing, beg in row 2 of lower 10-row B stripe, count 9 sts in from RH edge of dress (beg of RS rows) and work 12-st rep of Cat Chart in duplicate st a

total of 9 times around skirt, leaving a total of 9 B sts at LH edge of dress. Cont to work Cat Chart in this way until the 8 rows of duplicate st are complete. With B, embroider cat eyes with straight st (see photo).

ZIGZAG MOTIF

With RS facing, beg at RH edge of dress (beg RS rows) in row 1 of upper 10-row B stripe and work 18-st rep of Zigzag Chart in duplicate st as foll: beg with st 4 of chart, work to end of rep, work 18-st rep 5 times, work sts 1–15 once more. Cont to work Zigzag Chart in this way until the 10 rows of duplicate st are complete.

ASSEMBLY

With RS tog and matching the stripes,

sew center back seam from cast-on row to row 1 of Zigzag Chart. Fold hem to WS at turning ridge and sew cast-on edge to WS of skirt.

Sew sleeve seams and hems in same manner. Sew shoulder seams. Set sleeves into armholes.

Sew collar to neck edge of dress. Run black ribbon through eyelets on collar, trim to length needed, and tack down ends with needle and thread to secure. With A and crochet hook, work 1 row of sc along edges of back opening for bands. Sew snaps evenly spaced to bands. Attach decorative pin to collar if desired.

FRINGE

Cut 26 strands of A, each 6½"/16.5cm, for fringe. Hold 2 strands tog, fold them in

half, and with crochet hook, draw through each of the 7 zigzag points (st 10 on row 1 of Zigzag Chart). In same manner, attach 2 strands along center of both sleeves in each of the 3 A stripes (see photo).

HAT
With larger needles and 2 strands of A held tog, cast on 102 sts.
Note Hat is worked with 2 strands of A held tog, so that sts are intentionally tight to give the hat structure.

BRIM
Knit 3 rows.
Row 1 (RS) K1, [k2tog, k8] 10 times, k1—92 sts.
Row 2 and all WS rows Purl.
Row 3 K1, [k2tog, k7] 10 times, k1—82 sts.
Row 5 K1, [k2tog, k6] 10 times, k1—72 sts.
Row 7 K1, [k2tog, k5] 10 times, k1—62 sts.

Purl 3 rows for garter border. Knit 1 row.

SHAPE TOP POINT
Set-up row (WS) P30, place marker (pm), p2, pm, p30.
Row 1 (RS) K1, ssk, k to 2 sts before marker, ssk, sl marker, k2, sl marker, k2tog, k to last 3 sts, k2tog, k1—4 sts dec'd.
Row 2 and all WS rows Purl.
Rep rows 1 and 2 ten more times—18 sts. Remove markers.
Row 23 K1, [ssk] 4 times, [k2tog] 4 times, k1—10 sts.
Row 25 K1, [ssk] twice, [k2tog] twice, k1—6 sts.
Row 27 K1, ssk, k2tog, k1—4 sts.
Row 29 K1, k2tog, k1—3 sts.
Row 30 Sl 1, p2tog, psso. Fasten off last st.

ANGLED BRIM
With RS tog, fold hat along center decs.

Sew side edges tog beg at cast-on row. Turn RS out. Fold up sides of hat brim using photo as guide, block gently to shape.

BRIM DECORATION
With 3 strands of B held tog and crochet hook, make a chain long enough to fit around brim of hat just below garter border. Fasten off. Sew chain to brim under garter border.
Attach decorative pins to hat if desired (see photo).

SHOES (make 2)
With larger needles and 2 strands of A held tog, cast on 46 sts.
Note Shoes are worked with 2 strands of A held tog, so that sts are intentionally tight to give the shoes structure. Beg with a knit row, work in St st for 2 rows.

Dec row (RS) K1, ssk, k to last 3 sts, k2tog, k1—2 sts dec'd.
Purl 1 row.
Rep last 2 rows twice more—40 sts.
Dec row (RS) K1, [ssk] 3 times, k to last 7 sts, [k2tog] 3 times, k1—6 sts dec'd.
Purl 1 row.
Rep last 2 rows twice more—22 sts.
Work even in St st for 5 rows, ending with a RS row.
Knit 4 rows. Bind off.
With RS tog, fold boot in half. Sew side edges tog for front of boot, then seam along cast-on row for bottom of foot. Turn RS out. Weave light blue ribbon through front of shoe to look like shoelaces (see photo).

BELT

Use a watch band; OR cut buckle out of cardboard and paint gold. Cut length of ribbon and thread through buckle. ✳

ZIGZAG CHART

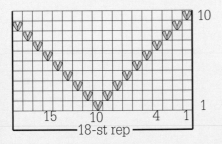

10

1

15   10   4   1
—18-st rep—

CAT CHART

8

1

12-st rep

COLOR KEY

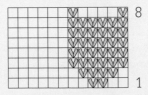

Ⓥ duplicate stitch (A)
☐ background (B)

NICKY'S WHIMSICAL RECIPE

Witches' Brooms

MAKES 18 BROOMS

INGREDIENTS

6 string cheese sticks, solid or two colors
18 pretzel sticks
Chives or green garden onions

DIRECTIONS

1. Cut each string cheese stick in thirds. Carefully press a pretzel stick into one side of each cheese stick about ½" deep.
2. Make the bristles by pulling the bottom of the cheese apart. Using sharp scissors, cut thin slices of chive that are about 4" in length.
3. Gently tie a chive around the top portion of the string cheese and snip off the long ends.
Enjoy!

79

Madame Vampire

● ● ● ○

"This Vampire's Taste Is Strange to Me
Her Favorite Drink Is Earl Grey Tea"

MATERIALS

- 2 1¾oz/50g spools (each approx 208yd/190m) of Bergère de France *Sirène* (polyamide) in #23087 requin (A–black) **1**
- 1 spool in #29528 tulipe (B–red)
- One pair size 4 (3.5mm) needles OR SIZE TO OBTAIN GAUGE
- Size E/4 (3.5mm) crochet hook
- 1yd/1m red sequins
- 5 snaps
- Sewing needle and thread
- 2 removable stitch markers
- 2 stitch holders
- ¼yd/.2m black felt or leather for crown
- 12"/30cm rhinestone fringe or decorative necklace
- ½yd/.4m black tulle for cape
- 3"/7.5cm of ¾" black satin ribbon for cape

GAUGE

26 sts and 38 rows to 4"/10cm over St st using size 4 (3.5mm) needles and 2 strands of yarn held tog.
TAKE TIME TO CHECK GAUGE.

STITCH GLOSSARY

CO1 (cast on 1—inc) Wrap yarn around left thumb from back to front. Insert RH needle from front into loop on thumb. Remove thumb from loop and tighten loop on needle (also called wrap cast-on)—1 stitch increased.

HERRINGBONE RIB

(multiple of 17 sts plus 4)
Row 1 (RS) P4, *CO1, k3, p2, p3tog, p2, k3, CO1, p4; rep from * to end.
Row 2 K4, *p4, k5, p4, k4; rep from* to end.
Row 3 P4, *CO1, k4, p1, p3tog, p1, k4, CO1, p4; rep from * to end.

Row 4 K4, *p5, k3, p5, k4; rep from* to end.
Row 5 P4, *CO1, k5, p3tog, k5, CO1, p4; rep from * to end.
Row 6 K4, *p6, k1, p6, k4; rep from* to end.
Rep rows 1–6 for herringbone rib.

DRESS

BACK

With 2 strands of A held tog, cast on 60 sts. Work in St st (knit on RS, purl on WS) until piece measures ½"/1.5cm from beg for hem, end with a RS row. Knit 1 row on WS for turning ridge. Cont in St st until piece measures 8"/20.5cm from turning ridge, end with a WS row.
Next row (RS) K8, [k2tog] 22 times, k8—38 sts.
DIVIDE BACK

Next row (WS) P19 for left back, join another 2 strands of A and p19 for right back. Work both sides of back at once as foll:
Next row (RS) On right side of back, k15, [p1, k1] twice; on left side of back, [k1, p1] twice, k15.
Next row (WS) On left side of back, p15, [k1, p1] twice; on right side of back, [p1, k1] twice, p15.
Cont in St st and rib as established until back measures 1½"/4cm above dec row, end with a WS row.

SHAPE ARMHOLE

Bind off 2 sts from each armhole edge once, then 1 st once—16 sts each side. Work even in pats as established until armhole measures 2½"/6.5cm, end with a WS row. Bind off.

FRONT

With 2 strands of A held tog, cast on 14 sts; with 2 strands of B held tog, cast on 32 sts; with second 2 strands of A, cast on 14 sts—60 sts.
Note When changing colors, twist yarns on WS to prevent holes in work. Cont with colors as established in St st until piece measures ½"/1.5cm from beg for hem, end with a RS row. Knit 1 row on WS for turning ridge. Cont with colors as established in St st until piece measures 8"/20.5cm from turning ridge, end with a WS row.
Next row (RS) K7 A, [k2tog with A] 3 times, k1 A; [k2tog with B] 16 times; k1 A, [k2tog with A] 3 times, k7 A—38 sts; 16 B sts in center and 11 A sts on each side.
Work even until front measures 1½"/4cm above dec row, end with WS row.

SHAPE ARMHOLE

Bind off 2 sts from each armhole edge once, then 1 st once—32 sts; 16 B sts in center and 8 A sts on each side. Work even until armhole measures 1½"/4cm, end with WS row.

SHAPE NECK

Next row (RS) K8 A and place removable marker on last A st worked, bind off 16 sts and cut B, knit to end with A and place removable marker on first A st worked. Cont on 8 sts each side with A until armhole measures 2½"/6.5cm, end with a WS row. Bind off.

SLEEVES (make 2)

With 2 strands of B held tog, cast on 44 sts. Work in St st for ½"/1.5cm from beg for hem, end with a RS row. Knit 1 row on WS for turning ridge. Cont in St st for 2 more rows. Change to 2 strands of A. Work in St st until piece measures ½"/1.5cm from turning ridge, end with a WS row.

Next row (RS) K1, k2tog, k to last 3 sts, ssk, k1—2 sts dec'd.

Purl 1 row. Rep last 2 rows 7 more times—28 sts. Work even until sleeve measures 4"/10cm from turning ridge, end with WS row.

SHAPE SLEEVE CAP

Bind off 2 sts at beg of next 2 rows and 1 st at beg of next 2 rows—22 sts. Work even until sleeve cap measures 1½"/4cm above first bind-off, end with WS row.

Next row (RS) Ssk, k to last 2 sts, k2tog—2 sts dec'd.

Purl 1 row. Rep last 2 rows once more—18 sts.

Next row (RS) [K3tog] 6 times across—6 sts. Bind off purlwise.

REMOVABLE COLLAR

With 2 strands of B held tog, cast on 55 sts. Rep rows 1–6 of herringbone rib twice.

Next row (RS) [K2tog] 27 times, k1—28 sts. Knit 1 row. Bind off.

FINISHING

Sew shoulder seams over first 8 sts from armhole edges, leaving rem sts at back neck open. Sew side seams, including hems. Sew sleeve seams and hems. Fold hems to WS and sew in place. Set in sleeves. With RS facing, sew one snap half at both front neck markers, the other snap half to WS of collar at both ends of bind-off row. With sewing needle and thread, sew 3 snaps to ribbed back bands, evenly spaced.

BODICE DECORATION

With A and crochet hook, make a chain approx 36"/91.5cm long. Using photo as guide, attach chain to bodice at both sides of B center panel at decrease row. Criss-cross the chain over B center panel like a shoelace, secure into the first black st on each side. Sew sequins to dress front from turning ridge to neck edge along both sides of B center panel.

CROWN

Using template on page 116, cut crown shape from felt or leather. Embellish with rhinestone fringe or necklace and purchased bat. Attach snap to ends to secure around doll's head.

CAPE

Cut toile to 12" x 20". Fold in half (fold is bottom hem). Sew top edges together with running stitch, ⅛" down. Gather to 3"/7.5cm and secure threads. Optional: fold satin ribbon in half over gathers and sew in place to secure. Cape fits under collar. ✳

Dream Genie

●●●○

"The Genie Makes Your Wish Come True
Just Rub the Lamp…She'll Come to You"

MATERIALS
- 2 .88oz/25g cones (each approx 109yd/100m) of Plymouth *Gold Rush* (viscose/metallized polyester) in #0043 purple (A) and #0056 pink (B) ②
- 1 cone in #0002 gold (C)
- One pair size 3 (3.25mm) needles OR SIZE TO OBTAIN GAUGE
- Size D/3 (3.25mm) crochet hook
- 3 snaps
- 10"/25.5cm of ¼"/.5cm elastic
- 1 decorative rhinestone or button for center of hat
- 1 string of small pearls, approx 30"/76cm long
- 1 white feather
- 1 decorative button for center of camisole neck
- Approx 18"/46cm of sequined tape to match color A for bolero
- 11"/28cm of decorative fringed tape for pantaloon waist
- Sewing needle and thread
- Stitch holders or safety pins

GAUGE
28 sts and 38 rows to 4"/10cm over St st (knit on RS, purl on WS) using size 3 (3.25) needles.
TAKE TIME TO CHECK GAUGE.

K1, P1 RIB
(over an even number of sts)
Row 1 (RS) *K1, p1; rep from * to end.
Row 2 K the knit sts and p the purl sts.
Rep row 2 for k1, p1 rib.

CAMISOLE
With B, cast on 75 sts.
Work 4 rows in St st.

TWISTED EDGING
Next row (RS) [K5, twist rem sts 360 degrees around the needle] 15 times.
Purl 1 row.

ADD BACK PLACKET
Next row (RS) Cast on 4 sts, [k1, p1] twice over these sts, knit to end—79 sts.
Next row Cast on 4 sts, [p1, k1] twice over these sts, purl to last 4 sts, work 4 sts in rib as established—83 sts.
Cont in St st, and rib first and last 4 sts as established for placket, until piece

measures approx 2½"/6.5cm from beg, end with a RS row.

GARTER ST BORDER
Next row (WS) Rib 4 sts, knit to last 4 sts, rib 4 sts.
Rep last row 4 more times.

DIVIDE FOR FRONT AND BACKS
Next row (RS) Bind off 28 sts for left back, k5 and place on a holder for strap, bind off next 17 sts for front, k5 and place on a holder for strap, bind off to end—28 sts for right back. Fasten off.

SHOULDER STRAPS
Sl 5 sts from holder to needle, ready for a RS row.
Row 1 (RS) Join B [k1, p1] twice, k1.
Row 2 [P1, k1] twice, p1.
Rep last 2 rows for 2½"/6.5cm. Bind off. Rep for other strap.

FINISHING
Sew 3 snaps evenly spaced to ribbed placket. Fold straps to back and sew in place. With B and tapestry needle, beg at center front of bound-off edge and run yarn through sts on WS for 1"/cm, gather slightly. Sew button to top border at the gather.

BOLERO
With C, cast on 54 sts. Knit 1 row, purl 1 row. Cont in St st, inc 1 st each side every other row 5 times—64 sts. Work even until back measures 1¾"/4.5cm from beg, end with a WS row.

DIVIDE FOR FRONTS AND BACK

Next row (RS) K 13 right front sts and sl to holder, bind off 4 sts for right armhole, knit until there are 30 sts on needle and sl to a holder for back, bind off 4 sts for left armhole, knit to end—13 left front sts.

LEFT FRONT

Working on 13 sts for left front, cont in St st until armhole measures ½"/1.5cm, end with a RS row.

SHAPE NECK

Next row (WS) Bind off 1 st, purl to end—12 sts.
Next row Knit.
Repeat last two rows 3 more times—9 sts.
Bind off.

RIGHT FRONT

Sl 13 right front sts to needle, ready for WS row. Join C and work in St st until armhole measures ½"/1.5cm, end with a WS row.

SHAPE NECK

Next row (RS) Bind off 1 st, knit to end—12 sts.
Next row Purl.
Repeat last two rows 3 more times—9 sts.
Bind off.

BACK

Sl 30 back sts to needle, ready for a WS row. Join C and work in St st until armhole measures 1½"/4cm. Bind off.

SLEEVES

With C, cast on 26 sts.
Work 4 rows in k1, p1 rib.
Next row (RS) With B, knit.
Next row Purl.
Next row (RS) K1, [kfb] 24 times, k1—50 sts.
Cont in St st until sleeve measures 2"/5cm from beg, end with a WS row.
Next row (RS) K2, k2tog, [k2tog, k4] 7 times, k2tog, k2—41 sts.
Work even until sleeve measures 4"/10cm from beg, end with a RS row.

SHAPE CAP

Bind off 3 sts at beg of next 2 rows—35 sts.

Purl 1 row.
Next (dec) row (RS) Ssk, knit to last 2 sts, k2tog—33 sts.
Work even for ½"/1.5cm, end with a WS row.
Next row (RS) [K3tog] 11 times—11 sts.
Bind off.

FINISHING

Sew shoulder seams. Sew sleeve seams. Sew sleeves into armholes, centering the k3togs at shoulder seam. With crochet hook and A, work sc evenly around entire outer edge of bolero. Sew sequined tape around outer edge along the color change. Cut 2 tassels from the fringe and sew to both front edges.

PANTALOONS

LEGS (make 2)
With C, cast on 36 sts. Work 4 rows in k1, p1 rib.
Change to A.
Knit 1 row, purl 1 row.
Next row (RS) [K1, kfb] 18 times—54 sts.
Purl 1 row.
Cont in St st until piece measures 2"/5cm from beg, end with a WS row.
Next row (RS) [K4, k2tog] 8 times, k6—46 sts.
Work even until piece measures 7½"/19cm from beg, end with a WS row.

SHAPE CROTCH

Bind off 4 sts at beg of next 2 rows and 1 st at beginning of next 4 rows—34 sts.
Work 6 rows even.

BEGIN WAIST COLOR DETAIL

Next row (RS) With C, k2; with A, knit to last 2 sts; join second ball of C, k2.
Next row (WS) With C, p3; with A, purl to last 3 sts; with C, p3.
Next row (RS) With C, k4; with A, knit to last 4 sts; with C, k4.
Cont in this manner to work 1 more C st on both sides of A section every row 5 more times—9 C sts on each side, 16 A sts in center.
Next row (RS) With C, knit.
Cont with C only for ½"/1.5cm, end with a RS row.

Knit 1 row on WS for turning ridge.
Work in St st until ½"/1.5cm above turning ridge for waistband. Bind off.

FINISHING

Sew crotch seam and leg seams. Fold waistband to WS along turning ridge and sew in place, leaving small opening for elastic. Feed elastic through opening, into and around waistband to other side, secure elastic with sewing thread, and sew opening closed. Sew fringed tape around waistband.

TURBAN

With C, cast on 12 sts. Knit 1 row, purl 1 row.
Next (inc) row (RS) [Kfb] in each st across—24 sts.
Purl 1 row.
Rep last 2 rows once more—48 sts.
Work 6 rows even in St st. Fasten off C.

BEGIN FLUTING

Row 1 (RS) [K6 A, k6 B] 4 times.
Row 2 (WS) K6 B, [k6 A, k6 B] 3 times, pulling yarn tightly on WS when stranding to create fluted pat, k6 A. First and last stripes are not fluted.
Rep rows 1 and 2 until fluted section measures 12"/30.5cm. Fasten off A and B.
With C, work 6 rows in St st.
Next row (RS) [K2tog] across—24 sts.
Purl 1 row.
Rep last 2 rows once more—12 sts.
Knit 2 rows. Bind off.

FINISHING

Sew cast-on edge to bound-off edge for front of turban. Sew left side edge (end of RS rows) tog for top of turban and gather along the B section only. Gather front seam tightly from front edge to last fluted A section.
Sew feather and decorative button to center front. Cut a tassel from the fringe, and sew below the button at center front.
Fold the string of pearls in half, fold in half again, wrap the sewing thread around the strands to hold them together at the folds. Sew one fold behind center front button, sew the other fold to center back of turban, at the top A stripe. Use photo as guide. ✳

Guardian Angel

"The Angel Floats Above the Sky
A Watchful Twinkle in Her Eye"

MATERIALS
- 1 .88oz/25g ball (each approx 109yd/100m) of Rowan *Anchor Artiste Metallic* (viscose/metallized polyester) in #301 silver (A) ⓪
- 3 .88oz/25g balls (each approx 180yd/165m) of Be Sweet *Grace + Style* (mohair/rayon bamboo/metallic) in silver (B) ④
- One pair size 4 (3.5mm) needles OR SIZE TO OBTAIN GAUGE
- Spare size 4 (3.5mm) needle
- 3 stitch holders
- 3 small snaps
- 22 ¼" (8mm) pearls
- 16"/40cm of ¼"/.5cm silver ribbon
- One pair feather wings
- Decorated silver craft wire for halo
- Sewing needle and thread.

GAUGE
24 sts and 28 rows to 4"/10cm over St st (knit on RS, purl on WS) using size 4 (3.5mm) needles.
TAKE TIME TO CHECK GAUGE.

LACE PATTERN
(multiple of 23 sts)
Row 1 (RS) K8, k2tog, yo, k1, p1, k1, yo, ssk, k8.
Row 2 P7, p2tog tbl, p2, yo, k1, yo, p2, p2tog, p7.
Row 3 K6, k2tog, k1, yo, k2, p1, k2, yo, k1, ssk, k6.
Row 4 P5, p2tog tbl, p3, yo, p1, k1, p1, yo, p3, p2tog, p5.
Row 5 K4, k2tog, k2, yo, k3, p1, k3, yo, k2, ssk, k4.

Row 6 P3, p2tog tbl, p4, yo, p2, k1, p2, yo, p4, p2tog, p3.
Row 7 K2, k2tog, k3, yo, k4, p1, k4, yo, k3, ssk, k2.
Row 8 P1, p2tog tbl, p5, yo, p3, k1, p3, yo, p5, p2tog, p1.
Row 9 K2tog, k4, yo, k5, p1, k5 yo, k4, ssk.
Row 10 P11, k1, p11.
Row 11 K11, p1, k11.
Row 12 P11, k1, p11.
Rep rows 1–12 for lace pat.

3-NEEDLE JOIN
With RS of skirts facing you and the needles parallel, *insert 3rd needle knitwise into first st of each needle and knit them together; rep from * until all sts are joined.

3-NEEDLE BIND-OFF
1. Hold right sides of pieces together on two needles. Insert 3rd needle knitwise into first st of each needle, and wrap yarn knitwise.
2. Knit these 2 sts together, and slip them off the needles. *Knit the next 2 sts together in the same manner.
3. Slip first st on 3rd needle over 2nd st and off needle. Rep from * in step 2 across row until all sts are bound off.

INNER SKIRT
With A, cast on 184 sts. Knit 1 row. Cut A, join B.

BEGIN LACE PAT
Row 1 (RS) Work 23-st rep of lace pat 8 times across.
Cont to work lace pat in this manner until row 12 is complete. Rep rows 1–12 once more. Work in St st until skirt measures 10"/25.5cm, measured from the lowest edge of the scallop, end with a WS row.

ADD BACK PLACKET FOR SNAPS
Next row (RS) Cast on 4 sts, [k1, p1] twice over these sts, k184—188 sts.
Next row (WS) Cast on 4 sts, [p1, k1] twice over these sts, p184, [k1, p1] twice—192 sts.
Next row [K1, p1] twice, k184, [p1, k1] twice.
Next row [P1, k1] twice, p184, [k1, p1] twice.

Rep last 2 rows until piece measures 11¼"/28.5cm, end with a WS row. Set work aside on spare needle.

OUTER SKIRT

Work as for inner skirt until outer skirt measures 6½"/16.5cm, end with a WS row.

JOIN SKIRTS

With RS of both skirts facing you and B, place outer skirt on top of inner skirt.

Next row (RS) Work first 4 sts of inner skirt, work 3-needle join over 184 sts of both skirts, work last 4 sts of inner skirt—192 sts.

BODICE

Next row (WS) [P1, k1] twice, [p2tog] 92 times, [k1, p1] twice—100 sts.

Next row With A [k1, p1] twice, [k2tog] 46 times, [p1, k1] twice—54 sts. Knit 2 rows.

DIVIDE FOR FRONT AND BACKS

Next row (WS) With A, [p1, k1] twice, k9 for right back, bind off 4 sts for right armhole, knit until 20 sts are on RH needle for front, bind off 4 sts for left armhole, work to end of row—13 sts for left back.

LEFT BACK

Row 1 (inc RS) With B [k1, p1] twice, [kfb] 9 times—22 sts.

Rows 2 and 4 P18, [k1, p1] twice.

Row 3 [K1, p1] twice, k18.

Row 5 (dec) With A [k1, p1] twice, k2tog [9 times]—13 sts.

Row 6 K9, [k1, p1] twice.

Rep rows 1–6 once more, then rep rows 1–4 once—22 sts.

SHAPE NECK

Row 5 (RS) With A, bind off 3 sts—1 st rem on RH needle; [k2tog, bind off 1] twice, k2tog to end of row—8 sts.

Row 6 Knit.

Next row Bind off 2 sts. Place rem 6 sts on holder for left shoulder.

FRONT

Place 20 front sts on needle, ready for a RS row.

Row 1 (inc RS) With B, [kfb] 20 times—40 sts.

Rows 2 and 4 Purl.

Row 3 Knit.

Row 5 (dec) With A, [k2tog] 20 times—20 sts.

Row 6 Knit.

Rep rows 1–6 once more, then rep rows 1 and 2 once—40 sts.

SHAPE NECK

Left front

Row 3 (RS) With B, k16 for left front, place next 8 sts on holder for front neck—16 sts rem for right front. Turn.

Row 4 P2tog, purl to end—15 sts.

Row 5 With A, [k2tog] 7 times, k1—8 sts.

Row 6 Bind off 2 sts, place rem 6 sts on holder for left front shoulder.

Right front

Place 16 sts for right front on needle, ready for a RS row.

Row 3 (RS) With B, k16.

Row 4 Purl to last 2 sts, p2tog—15 sts.

Row 5 With A, k1, [k2tog] 7 times—8 sts.

Row 6 Knit.

Next row Bind off 2 sts, place rem 6 sts on holder for right front shoulder.

RIGHT BACK

Place 13 sts for right back on needle, ready for a RS row.

Row 1 (inc RS) With B, [kfb] 9 times, [p1, k1] twice—22 sts.

Rows 2 and 4 [K1, p1] twice, p18.

Row 3 K18, [p1, k1] twice.

Row 5 (dec) With A, [k2tog] 9 times, [k1, p1] twice—13 sts.

Row 6 [K1, p1] twice, k9.

Rep rows 1–6 once more, then rep rows

1–5 once—13 sts.

SHAPE NECK

Row 6 (WS) With A, bind off 5 sts, work to end—8 sts.

Next row Knit.

Next row Bind off 2 sts, place rem 6 sts on holder for right back shoulder. With RS tog, join shoulders using 3-needle bind-off method.

COLLAR

With RS facing and A, beg at left back edge, pick up and k 14 sts along left neck, k 8 sts from front holder, pick up and k 14 sts along right neck—36 sts. Knit 2 rows. Bind off loosely.

SLEEVES

With A, cast on 46 sts. Knit 1 row. Cut A, join B.

BEGIN LACE PAT

Row 1 (RS) Work 23-st rep of lace pat twice across.

Cont to work lace pat in this manner until row 12 is complete.

Next row (RS) K2tog, knit to last 2 sts, ssk—44 sts.

Cont in St st and rep dec row every 4th row 5 more times—34 sts.

Work even until sleeve measures 5"/12.5cm from the lowest edge of the scallop, end with a WS row.

Next row (RS) K10, [k2tog] 7 times, k10—27 sts. Bind off loosely.

FINISHING

Sew sleeve seams, set in sleeves. Sew back seam on underskirt only. Sew snaps to back opening. Using photo as a guide, sew a pearl to the center of each lace repeat on the cast-on row of both skirts and sleeves. Tie the ribbon in a bow, sew a pearl to the center, then sew ribbon to center of front on the first A stripe. Wrap silver wire into a circle to fit top of doll's head for halo. ✳

Monster Mash

"These Monsters May Look Wild and Mean
But They Are Truly Quite Serene"

●●●○

MATERIALS
- 2 1¾oz/50g balls (each approx 27yd/25m) of Lion Brand *Romance* (nylon/polyester) in #144 sachet (J) OR #157 lemon yellow (6)
- 1 package of 8 .35oz/10g skeins (each approx 28yd/26m) of Lion Brand *Bonbons* (acrylic) in #610 Brights Collection in pink (A), orange-red (B), purple (C), lime (D), orange (E), turquoise (F), magenta (G), and yellow (H) (2)
- One pair each sizes 5 and 8 (3.75 and 5mm) needles OR SIZE TO OBTAIN GAUGE
- One spare size 5 (3.75mm) needle for 3-needle join
- Two ⅜"/9mm squiggle eyes and glue
- Yarn needle
- Small amount of polyester stuffing
- 4 snaps
- Sewing needle and thread
- Stitch holders
- 10 removable stitch markers

GAUGE
24 sts and 32 rows to 4"/10cm over St st using smaller needles and *Bonbons*.
TAKE TIME TO CHECK GAUGE.

SEED STITCH
(over any number of sts)
Row 1 (RS) *K1, p1; rep from * to end.
Row 2 K the purl sts and p the knit sts.
Rep row 2 for seed st.

K2, P2 RIB
(multiple of 4 sts plus 2)
Row 1 (RS) *K2, p2; rep from * to last 2 sts, k2.

Row 2 K the knit sts and p the purl sts.
Rep row 2 for k2, p2 rib.

3-NEEDLE JOIN
With RS of layers facing you and the needles parallel, *insert 3rd needle knitwise in the first st on each needle and knit them tog: rep from * until all sts are joined.

STITCH GLOSSARY
CO1 (cast on 1—inc) Wrap yarn around left thumb from back to front. Insert RH needle from front into the loop on thumb. Remove thumb from loop and tighten loop on needle (also called wrap cast-on). 1 stitch has been increased.

NOTE
Dress is worked in one piece, joining ruffles as they are worked, to the armholes. The back is seamed to the waist in finishing and ribbed bands are added to the open back edges for snap closure.

DRESS
FIRST RUFFLE
With smaller needles and A, cast on 106 sts.
Work in seed st for 1¼"/3cm, end with a WS row.
Dec row (RS) K4, *k2tog; rep from * to last 4 sts, k4 —57 sts.
Next row Purl, placing markers at each end of row.
Change to B and work in St st (k on RS, p on WS) until piece measures 2½"/6.5cm from beg, end with a WS row. Cut yarn and leave sts on spare needle.

SECOND RUFFLE

With smaller needles and C, cast on 106 sts. Knit 2 rows.

Beg with a RS row, work even in St st stripes as foll: 2 rows D, 2 rows E, 2 rows F, 2 rows G.

Dec row (RS) With H, k4, *k2tog; rep from * to last 4 sts, k4—57 sts.

Next row Purl, placing markers at each end of row.

Joining row (RS) With RS facing you and H, hold second ruffle in front of first ruffle and join, using 3-needle join—57 sts. Cont in St st and H until second ruffle measures 2½"/6.5cm from beg, end with a WS row. Do *not* cut yarn, leave sts on spare needle.

THIRD RUFFLE

With smaller needles and F, cast on 106 sts. Work in seed st for 1¼"/3cm, end with a WS row.

Dec row (RS) K4, *k2tog; rep from * to last 4 sts, k4—57 sts.

Next row Purl, placing markers at each end of row.

Joining row (RS) With H, join as for previous ruffle, holding third ruffle in front of second ruffle— 57 sts. Purl 1 row.

BEGIN TOP

Work in St st and stripe pattern as follows: 2 rows H, 4 rows C.

Row 1 (RS) K1 D, *k1 C, k1 D; rep from * to end. Cut C.

Rows 2–4 With D, work in St st.

Row 5 K1 D, *k1 G, k1 D; rep from * to end. Cut D.

Rows 6–8 With G, work in St st.

DIVIDE FOR FRONT AND BACK

Next row (RS) Cont with G, k 13 sts and place on st holder for left back, bind off next 2 sts for left armhole, k until 27 sts from bind-off and place these 27 sts on holder for front, bind off next 2 sts for right armhole, k to end—13 sts for right back.

RIGHT BACK

Next row (WS) Working on 13 right back sts, purl.

Next (dec) row Ssk, k to end—12 sts. Place marker on ssk.

Work even with G in St st on 12 sts for right back until armhole measures 2½"/6.5cm, end with a WS row. Bind off.

LEFT BACK

Place 13 left back sts on needle, ready for a WS row.

Next row (WS) With G, purl.

Next (dec) row K to last 2 sts, k2tog— 12 sts. Place marker on k2tog.

Work even with G in St st on 12 sts for left back until armhole measures 2½"/6.5cm, end with a WS row. Bind off.

FRONT

Place 27 front sts on needle, ready for a WS row.

Next row (WS) Purl.

Next (dec) row Ssk, knit to last 2 sts, k2tog—25 sts. Place markers on ssk and on k2tog.

Work even with G in St st until armhole measures 1¼"/3cm.

Work in stripe pat as foll: 2 rows E, 2 rows D, end with a WS row. Cut yarn, join C.

SHAPE NECK

Next row (RS) K9 C, join a 2nd ball of C and bind off center 7 sts, k to end—9 sts each side of neck.

Next row (WS) Purl across each side of neck.

Next (dec) row Knit across left side of neck to last 2 sts, k2tog; on right side of neck ssk, knit to end—8 sts rem each side for shoulder. Work even in St st until armhole measures 2½"/6.5cm, end with a WS row. Bind off.

FINISHING

Matching the row markers, sew back seam of each ruffle up to the last F row of third ruffle, leaving back of top open. Sew shoulder seams over first 8 sts from armhole edges, leaving rem 4 sts at back neck open for neck fringe.

NECK FRINGE

With smaller needles and E, cast on 10 sts.

Rows 1 and 2 Knit.

Row 3 Bind off 7 sts, k to end—3 sts.

Row 4 K3, cast on 7 sts.

Rep rows 1–4 for 13 more times, then rep rows 1 and 2 once more—15 fringes.

Bind off.

Sew around neck opening.

ARMHOLE FRINGE

(Make 2: 1 each in B and H)

Work as for neck fringe until 10 fringes are complete, then rep rows 1 and 2 once more—11 fringes. Bind off. Pin center of fringe to shoulder seam, then cast-on and bound-off ends to the armhole decrease markers. Sew fringe to armhole edge between markers, leaving lower part of armhole opening plain.

BACK BANDS

With smaller needle, RS facing and B, pick up and k 30 sts along right back opening, excluding neck fringe. Work in k2, p2, rib for ½"/1cm. Bind off. Rep for left back band. Overlap and sew side edges of bands tog at top of third ruffle. Sew snaps to bands.

BOBBLES

(make 6: 1 each in B, C, D, E, F, and H)

Make a slip knot and place on smaller needle.

Row 1 (RS) Alternate knitting into front and back of slip knot until there are 5 sts on needle.

Rows 2–4 Work in St st.

Row 5 Ssk, k1, k2tog—3 sts.

Row 6 Sl 1, p2tog, psso. Fasten off rem st. Sew bobbles to top of dress, using photo as guide.

WRIST CUFFS (make 2)

With smaller needles and C, cast on 22 sts. Knit 2 rows. Work 5 two-row stripes in St st in colors as desired. With C, knit 2 rows. Bind off. Sew side edges tog to form cuff.

LEGGINGS (make 2)

Note This yarn can be slippery; be sure to insert needle completely into st to avoid dropping sts.

With larger needles and J, cast on 17 sts. Work in St st for 3"/7.5cm. Bind off loosely, fasten off securely. Mark "fluffier" side as RS. With RS tog, fold piece in half lengthwise and sew side edges tog to form leggings.

FUR HOOD

With larger needles and J, cast on 66 sts.

Row (dec) 1 K1, k2tog, k to last 3 sts, k2tog, k1—64 sts.
Row (dec) 2 P1, p2tog, p to last 3 sts, p2tog, p1—62 sts.
Rep rows 1 and 2 for 3 more times—50 sts. Work even in St st until piece measures 4"/10cm from beg. Bind off loosely, fasten off last st securely. Mark "fluffier" side as RS. With RS tog, fold hood in half lengthwise and sew up the bound-off edge for back seam.

EYES (make 2)
With smaller needles and G, cast on 8 sts, leaving a long tail for seaming.
Row 1 (inc RS) *Kfb; rep from * to last st, k1—15 sts.
Row 2 and all WS rows Purl, matching color of previous row.
Rows 3, 5, 7, and 9 With D, knit.
Row (dec) 11 *K2tog; rep from * to last st, k1—8 sts.
Cut yarn, leaving a long tail of D. With yarn needle, thread tail through open sts and pull tight to close. Sew side edges together. Fill with stuffing. With yarn needle, thread cast-on tail through cast-on sts and gather, securing thread. Glue squiggle eyes to tops of eyes at cast-on edge.
Sew eyes to hood, using photo as guide.

HORNS (make 2)
With smaller needles and E, cast on 15 sts.
Rows 1–4 Work in St st.
Row (dec) 5 (RS) K1, ssk, k to last 3 sts, k2tog, k1—13 sts.
Rows 6–8 Work in St st. Cut E.
Row (dec) 9 With B, k1, ssk, k to last 3 sts, k2tog, k1—11 sts.
Rows 10–12 Work in St st.
Row 13 Rep row 9—9 sts.
Row 14 Work in St st.
Rows 15–18 Rep rows 13 and 14 twice—5 sts.
Row 19 K1, SK2P, k1—3 sts.
Row 20 SP2P. Fasten off last st.
Sew side seam and fill with stuffing. Sew horns to hood, using photo as guide. ✳

Monster Mash Kids' Hat & Wristlets

"A Kid-Size Monster Is Just as Scary—and Just as Cute!"

SIZE
One size, to fit child.

FINISHED MEASUREMENTS
WRISTLETS
Circumference approx 5½"/14cm
Length approx 3¼"/8cm

HOOD
Hood at widest point approx 14"/35.5cm
Hood length approx 15"/38cm

MATERIALS
- 3 1¾oz/50g balls (each approx 27yd/25m) of Lion Brand *Romance* (nylon/polyester) in #144 sachet (J) **6**
- 1 package of 8.35oz/10g skeins (each approx 28yd/26m) of Lion Brand *Bonbons* (acrylic), Brights Collection in pink (A), orange-red (B), purple (C), lime (D), orange (E), turquoise (F), magenta (G), yellow (H) **2**
- One pair each sizes 5 and 8 (3.75 and 5mm) needles OR SIZE TO OBTAIN GAUGE
- Two ⅝"/1.5cm squiggle eyes and glue
- Yarn needle
- Small amount of polyester stuffing
- Small crochet hook for fringe
- Glue

GAUGES
24 sts and 32 rows to 4"/10cm over St st using size 5 (3.75mm) needles and *Bonbons*.
12 sts to 4"/cm over St st using size 8 (5mm) needles and *Romance*. Row gauge does not matter. Fabric will stretch over time.
TAKE TIME TO CHECK GAUGES.

WRISTLETS (make 2)
Note Leave a 3"/7.5cm tail at beg and end of each color for fringe.
With smaller needles and C, cast on 32 sts. Knit 2 rows. Cont in St st (k on RS, p on WS), work 11 2-row stripes in colors as desired. With C, knit 2 rows. Bind off. Sew side edges tog to form tube.

FRINGE
Secure tails in seam on WS, then pull remaining length through to RS with crochet hook. Trim fringe to even length.

FUR HOOD
Note This yarn can be slippery; be sure to insert needle completely into st to avoid dropping it.
With larger needles and J, cast on 102 sts.
Row 1 (dec) K1, k2tog, k to last 3 sts, k2tog, k1—100 sts.
Row 2 (dec) P1, p2tog, p to last 3 sts, p2tog, p1—98 sts.
Rep last 2 rows 5 more times—78 sts. Work even in St st until 7"/18cm from beg. Bind off loosely, fasten off last st securely. Mark "fluffier" side as RS. With RS tog, fold hood in half lengthwise and sew the bound-off edge for back seam.

EYES (make 2)
With smaller needles and G, cast on 10 sts, leaving a long tail for seaming.
Row 1 (inc RS) *Kfb; rep from * to last st, k1—19 sts.
Row 2 and all WS rows Purl.
Rows 3 and 5 Knit.
Rows 7, 9, 11, 13, and 15 With D, knit.
Row (dec) 17
*K2tog; rep from * to last st, k1—10 sts. Cut yarn, leaving a long tail of D. With yarn needle, thread tail through open sts and pull tight to close.
Sew side edges together. Fill with stuffing.
With yarn needle, thread cast-on tail through cast-on sts and gather, securing thread.
Glue squiggle eyes to tops of eyes at cast-on edge.
Sew eyes to hood, using photo as guide.

HORNS
With smaller needles and E, cast on 23 sts.
Rows 1–10 Work in St st.
Row 11 (dec RS) K1, ssk, k to last 3 sts, k2tog, k1—21 sts.
Row 12 Work in St st. Cut E.
Row 13 (dec) With B, k1, ssk, k to last 3 sts, k2tog, k1—19 sts.
Rows 14–16 Work in St st.
Row 17 Rep rows 13—17 sts.
Row 18 Work in St st.
Rows 19–30 Rep rows 17 and 18 six times—5 sts.
Row 31 K1, SK2P, k1—3 sts.
Row 32 SK2P. Fasten off last st.
Sew side seam and fill with stuffing. Sew horns to hood, using photo as guide. ✻

Flower Fairy

"Flower Fairies Can Create Blossoms That Will Captivate"

●●●●

MATERIALS
- 1 1¾oz/50g hank (each approx 98yd/90m) of Berroco *Captiva* (cotton/polyester/acrylic) each in #5558 orchid (A), #5541 seedling (B), #5557 thistle (C), and #5512 aqua (D) ④
- One pair size 7 (4.5mm) needles OR SIZE TO OBTAIN GAUGE
- Spare size 7 (4.5mm) needle
- Size 7 (4.5mm) crochet hook for provisional cast-on
- Scrap yarn of similar weight
- Stitch markers
- Stitch holders
- 5 small snaps
- 1 large snap
- 1 yd/1m glitter tulle in lavender
- Approx 3 dozen ½" (13mm) silk roses in blue, pink, and purple
- 12"/30.5cm of short beaded fringe in a corresponding color for headband
- 1½yd of ½"/ 1.5cm satin ribbon in green
- Small amount of mixed beads and pearls in coordinating colors
- Purchased wings
- Sewing needle and thread
- Glue

GAUGE
22 sts and 26 rows to 4"/10cm over St st (knit on RS, purl on WS) using size 7 (4.5mm) needles. TAKE TIME TO CHECK GAUGE.

STITCH GLOSSARY
Kbf Knit into back and front of same st to inc 1 st.
Kfb Knit into front and back of same st to inc 1 st.

CO1 (cast on 1—inc) Wrap yarn around left thumb from back to front. Insert RH needle from front into the loop on thumb. Remove thumb from loop and tighten loop on needle (also called wrap cast-on). 1 stitch has been increased.

PROVISIONAL CAST-ON
Using scrap yarn and crochet hook, chain the number of sts to cast on, plus a few extra. Cut a tail and pull the tail through the last chain. With knitting needle and yarn, pick up and knit the stated number of sts through the "purl bumps" on the back of the chain. To remove scrap chain, when instructed, pull out the tail from the last crochet st. Gently and slowly pull on the tail to unravel the crochet sts, carefully

placing each released knit st on a needle.

NOTES
1) Before beginning, wind off 2nd balls each of B, C, and D each approx 15yd/14m long to be used for skirt.
2) Dress is worked from the shoulders down.

DRESS
RIGHT FRONT
With scrap yarn, cast on 5 sts for shoulder, using provisional cast-on method.
Change to A.
Row 1 (RS) K5.
Row 2 P5.
Row 3 K4, kbf—6 sts.
Row 4 P6.
Row 5 K5, kbf—7 sts.
Row 6 P7.
Row 7 K6, kbf—8 sts.
Row 8 P8. Cut yarn and place these 8 sts on a st holder, ready for a RS row.

LEFT FRONT
With scrap yarn, cast on 5 sts for shoulder, using provisional cast-on method. Change to A.
Row 1 (RS) K5.
Row 2 P5.
Row 3 Kfb, k4—6 sts.
Row 4 P6.
Row 5 Kfb, k5—7 sts.
Row 6 P7.
Row 7 Kfb, k6—8 sts.
Row 8 P8.

JOIN FRONTS
Row 9 (RS) K8 from right front holder, cast on 5 sts, k8 from left front

holder—21 sts.

Rows 10–14 Work in St st. Place sts on holder for front, ready for a RS row.

LEFT BACK
Remove scrap yarn from left front and with RS facing, place sts on needle ready for a RS row. Join A, place remov-able marker on row to indicate shoulder.

Row 1 (RS) K5, cast on 8 sts—13 sts.

Row 2 (WS) K1, p1, k1, p10.

Row 3 K10, p1, k1, p1.

Row 4 K1, p1, k1, p10.

Rows 5–14 Rep rows 3 and 4 five more times.

Cut yarn and place sts on a holder.
RIGHT BACK
Remove scrap yarn from right front and with WS facing, place sts on needle ready for a WS row. Join A, place remov-able marker on row to indicate shoulder.

Row 1 (WS) P5, cast on 8 sts—13 sts.

Row 2 (RS) P1, k1, p1, k10.

Row 3 P10, k1, p1, k1.
Rows 4–13 Rep rows 2 and 3 five more times.

JOIN BACKS AND FRONT
Row 1 (RS) P1, k1, p1, k 10 right back sts; cast on 6 sts for right underarm; k 21 sts from front holder; cast on 6 sts for left underarm; k10, p1, k1, p1 left back sts—59 sts.

BODICE
Row 2 (WS) K1, p1, k1, p to last 3 sts, k1, p1, k1.
Row 3 P1, k1, p1, k to last 3 sts, p1, k1, p1.
Rows 4–17 Rep rows 2 and 3 seven more times.
Row 18 Rep row 2.
Row 19 (RS) Bind off 2 sts, work until there are 7 sts on RH needle, CO1, [k7, CO1] twice, k6, CO1, [k7, CO1] 3 times, k6, p1, k1, p1—64 sts.
Row 20 Bind off 2 sts, purl to last st, k1. Cut A—62 sts.

SKIRT
Row 1 (RS) With B, p1, *[work row 1 of skirt chart] twice; with C, [work row 1 of skirt chart] twice; with D, [work row 1 of skirt chart] twice; rep from * once more, p1 D.
Row 2 With D, k1, *[work row 2 of skirt chart] twice; with C, [work row 1 of skirt chart] twice; with B, [work row 2 of skirt chart] twice; rep from * once more, k1 B.
Cont as established until row 18 of skirt chart is complete, AT SAME TIME, bind off first st of row 18—169 sts.

POINTS
(Each point worked separately, 2 points over each color section)
First point With B, bind off first st of row,
**work row 1 of point chart, turn and leave rem sts on needle—12 sts for point. Use spare needle to work row 2 of chart—12 sts.
When chart row 13 is complete, fasten off last st. Rep from ** for all rem points, working in same colors as established.

SLEEVES
With C, cast on 60 sts.
Knit 2 rows. Beg with a RS row, work 10 rows in St st.
Next (dec) row (RS) [K3tog] 20 times—20 sts. Purl 1 row. Bind off.

FINISHING
NECKBAND
With RS facing and B, beg at left back edge, pick up and K 37 sts evenly along neck edge.
Row 1 (WS) *P1, k1; rep from * to last st, end p1.
Row 2 Knit the k sts and purl the p sts. Rep rows 1 and 2 once more. Bind off.

Fold bound-off edge of sleeve in half and mark the center, match to shoulder marker. Sew bound-off edge to each side of armhole, leaving side edge of sleeve open. Sew roses to points of skirt, around the waist and 1 to center of front neck, using photo as guide. Hang long beaded fringe from neck rose. Cut 2 lengths of ribbon, each 18"/45.5cm long, and make 2 bows. Sew one to back waist of dress, the other to the headband. Sew center back skirt seam, leave points unsewn. Sew 4 small snaps, evenly spaced, to back bodice opening.

CRINOLINE PETTICOAT

Cut the tulle into 4 strips, each 36"/97cm wide and 7"/18cm tall. Place the strips on top of each other and mark one long edge as the top.

GATHER TULLE
With sewing needle and thread, run 2 lines of sts, one at ⅛"/3mm and one at ½"/12mm from top edge, through all layers. With sharp scissors, cut points into lower edge of tulle, resembling skirt. Pull threads gently and gather to fit doll's waist, then secure the threads. Sew half a snap at both ends of gathered fabric to close waistband.

HEADBAND
With B, cast on 8 sts.
Row 1 (RS) [K1, p1] 4 times.
Row 2 Knit the k sts and purl the p sts. Rep rows 1 and 2 until piece measures approx 12"/30.5cm, or long enough to fit around your doll's head. Bind off.

FINISHING
Sew one half of large snap to each end. Sew or glue roses and beads to RS and short beaded fringe to length of WS, using photo as a guide.
Cut 1 piece of tulle, 36"/97cm wide and 2½"/6.5cm tall. With sewing needle and thread, run 2 lines of sts lengthwise down the center. Pull threads gently and gather to fit inside the headband, then secure the threads. Center on WS of headband and sew in place.

WAND (Optional)
Purchase a wand and sew a rose to center. Tie remaining half yard of ribbon to top of handle. ✱

SKIRT CHART

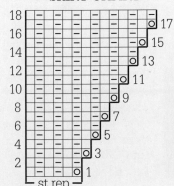

STITCH KEY

□	k on RS, p on WS
⊟	p on RS, k on WS
◯	yo
╱	k2tog on RS
╲	p2tog on RS, k2tog on WS
⋋	k3tog
⋌	p3tog

POINT CHART

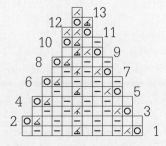

Magical Dragon

●●●●

*"A Dragon's Flame Can Really Do
A Good Job Lighting Barbecue"*

MATERIALS

- 1 1¾oz/50g ball (each approx 98yd/90m) of Crystal Palace Yarns | *Cotton Chenille* (cotton) each in #2214 bluebell (A), #9660 purple (B), and #2342 fern (C) (④)
- 1 3½oz/100g skein (each approx 94yd/86m) of Crystal Palace Yarns *Splash* (polyester) in #3734 violets are blue (D) (⑥)
- One pair each sizes 4 and 6 (3.5 and 4mm) needles OR SIZE TO OBTAIN GAUGE
- One set (4) each sizes 4 and 6 (3.5 and 4mm) double-pointed needles (dpns)
- Stitch markers
- Stitch holders
- Polyester stuffing for horns and tail
- Small amount of felt to secure stuffing in horns and tail
- ¼yd/.25m of gold leather or leather-like fabric for cuffs
- 4 small snaps
- ½yd/.5m red ribbon, ⅛"/32cm wide
- 2 big copper-colored beads for eyes
- 2 small red crystal beads for eyes
- Plastic eyelashes
- Glue
- Sewing needle and thread
- Yarn needle

GAUGE

14 sts and 32 rows to 4"/10cm over St st (knit on RS, purl on WS) using size 6 (4mm) needles and chenille yarn.
TAKE TIME TO CHECK GAUGE.

STITCH GLOSSARY

Kfbf Knit into front, back, then front of same st to inc 2 sts.

Kfbfbf Knit into front, back, front, back, and front of same st to inc 4 sts.
CO1 (cast on 1—increase) Wrap yarn around left thumb from back to front. Insert RH needle from front into the loop on thumb. Remove thumb from loop and tighten loop on needle (also called wrap cast-on). 1 stitch has been increased.

SHORT ROW WRAP AND TURN (W&T)

on RS row (on WS row)
1) Wyib (wyif), sl next st purlwise.
2) Move yarn between the needles to the front (back).

3) Sl the same st back to LH needle. Turn work. One st is wrapped.

NOTES

1) Horns, wings, and leg openings are identified as right and left as worn by doll.
2) See page 116 for template for cuffs, fastened with one snap each.

DRAGON HOOD

FRONT
With larger needles and A, cast on 42 sts.
Row 1 [K2, p2] 10 times, k2.
Row 2 [P2, k2] 10 times, p2.
Rep last 2 rows 3 more times.

SHAPE SNOUT
Row 9 (RS) K18, [k2tog] 3 times, k18—39 sts.
Row 10 P18, p3tog, p18—37 sts.
Row 11 (inc) K17, kfb, kfbf, kfb, k17—41 sts.
Row 12 P17, k2, p3, k2, p17.
Row 13 K17, p2, k3, p2, k17.
Rep last 2 rows until piece measures 3½"/9cm from beg, end with a WS row.

DIVIDE FOR HORNS
Next row (RS) Bind off 8 sts; knit until there are 8 sts on needle and place on a holder for left horn; k1, p2, k3, p2, k1 and place on a 2nd holder for hood; k8 for right horn; bind off 8 sts.

RIGHT HORN
Divide the 8 sts for right horn on 3 smaller dpns, place marker (pm) for beg of rnd. Change to B. Knit 4 rnds.
Rnd 5 (dec) [K2, k2tog] twice—6 sts.
Rnd 6 Knit.

Rnd 7 (dec) [K1, k2tog] twice—4 sts.
Rnd 8 Knit.
Rnd 9 (dec) [K2tog] twice—2 sts.
Bind off.
Work left horn in same manner.

HOOD TOP
Sl the 9 hood sts to larger needles, ready for a RS row.
Row 1 (RS) With A, pick up and knit 1 st behind left horn, then p3, k3, p3 hood sts, pick up and knit 1 st behind right horn—11 sts.
Row 2 K4, p3, k4.

SHAPE BACK OF HOOD
Row 3 (inc) Kfb, p3, k3, p3, kfb—13 sts.
Row 4 P the inc'd sts, k the knit sts, and p the purl sts.
Work as established, and inc at beg and end of the next 3 RS rows, working inc'd sts in rev St st (purl on RS, knit on WS)—19 sts.
Work even until piece measures 5½"/14cm from beg of hood, end with a WS row.

BACK
INCREASE FOR SHOULDERS
Next row (RS) CO1, work to end, CO1—21 sts.
Work as established, inc 1 st each side every RS row 3 more times—27 sts.
Work even until piece measures 8½"/21.5cm from beg of hood, place a marker at each end of row for belly attachment later.
Work even until piece measures 11"/28cm from beg of hood, end with a RS row.

TAIL BASE—RIGHT SIDE
With A, work rev St st short rows from WS as foll:
Row 1 (WS) K11, w&t, purl to end.
Row 2 K10, w&t, purl to end.
Row 3 K9, w&t, purl to end.
Row 4 K8, w&t, purl to end.
Row 5 K7, w&t, purl to end.
Row 6 K6, w&t, purl to end.
Row 7 K5, w&t, purl to end.
Row 8 K4, w&t, purl to end.
Row 9 K3, w&t, purl to end.
Row 10 K2, w&t, purl to end.
Row 11 K1, w&t, purl to end. Cut A.

TAIL BASE—LEFT SIDE
Join A, work rev St st short rows from RS as foll:
Row 1 (RS) P11, w&t, knit to end.
Row 2 P10, w&t, knit to end.
Row 3 P9, w&t, knit to end.
Row 4 P8, w&t, knit to end.
Row 5 P7, w&t, knit to end.
Row 6 P6, w&t, knit to end.
Row 7 P5, w&t, knit to end.
Row 8 P4, w&t, knit to end.
Row 9 P3, w&t, knit to end.
Row 10 P2, w&t, knit to end.
Row 11 P1, w&t, knit to end.
Divide sts over larger dpns for tail, pm for beg of rnd and join—27 sts. Hiding wraps as you go, work as established, with center 3 sts in St st and sts either side in rev St st, for 3"/7.5cm. Change to smaller dpns and B.

SHAPE TAIL TIP
Rnd 1 K27.
Rnd 2 (dec) K2tog, k to last 2 sts, ssk—25 sts.
Cont in St st (k every rnd) and rep dec rnd every 3rd rnd 9 more times—7 sts. Cut yarn, leaving a long tail, and thread tail through open sts to close.

SCALES
LARGE (make 3)
With C and larger needles, cast on 11 sts. Knit 2 rows. Bind off 1 st at beg of next 9 rows—2 sts.
Next row K2tog. Fasten off last st.

MEDIUM (make 4)
With C and larger needles, cast on 9 sts. Knit 2 rows. Bind off 1 st at beg of next 7 rows—2 sts.
Next row K2tog. Fasten off last st.

SMALL (make 4)
With C and larger needles, cast on 7 sts. Knit 2 rows. Bind off 1 st at beg of next 5 rows—2 sts.
Next row K2tog. Fasten off last st.

LEFT WING
With B and smaller needles, cast on 7 sts, leaving a long tail for sewing.
Row 1 (RS) K1, [p1, k1] 3 times.
Row 2 P1, [k1, p1] 3 times.
Row 3 (inc) K1, [p1, CO1, k1] 3 times—10 sts.
Row 4 P1, [k2, p1] 3 times.
Row 5 (inc) K1, [p2, CO1, k1] 3 times—13 sts.
Row 6 P1, [k3, p1] 3 times.
Row 7 (inc) K1, [p3, CO1, k1] 3 times—16 sts.
Row 8 P1, [k4, p1] 3 times.
Row 9 (inc) K1, [p4, CO1, k1] 3 times—19 sts.
Row 10 P1, [k5, p1] 3 times.
Rows 11 and 13 [K1, p5] 3 times, k1.
Rows 12 and 14 [P1, k5] 3 times, p1.
Row 15 Bind off 6 sts, work to end—13 sts.
Rows 16–18 K the knit sts and p the purl sts.
Row 19 Bind off 6 sts, work to end—7 sts.
Rows 20–22 K the knit sts and p the purl sts.
Bind off.

RIGHT WING
Work as for left wing through row 13.
Row 14 Bind off 6 sts, work to end—13 sts.
Rows 15–17 K the knit sts and p the purl sts.
Row 18 Bind off 6 sts, work to end—7 sts.
Rows 19–21 K the knit sts and p the purl sts.
Bind off.

BOBBLES
(make 7 with C, 5 with A)
With larger needles, cast on 1 st.
Row 1 (WS) Kfbfbf—5 sts.
Rows 2 and 4 Purl.
Row 3 Knit.
Row 5 K2tog, k1, k2tog—3 sts.
Row 6 Purl.
Row 7 SK2P. Fasten off.

BELLY
Note Belly is worked from the top down.
With D and larger needles, cast on 20 sts. Work in St st until piece measures 2½"/6.5cm from beg, end with a WS row.
Next row (RS) Kfb, knit to last st, kfb—22 sts.
Rep inc row every RS row 3 more times—28 sts.
Work even in St st until piece measures 6½"/16.5cm from beg, end with a WS row.

DIVIDE FOR LEG OPENINGS

Row 1 (RS) K8, bind off 4 sts for right leg opening, knit until there are 4 sts on RH needle for crotch, bind off 4 sts for left leg opening, knit to end—8 sts rem.
Row 2 P8, cast on 6 sts, p4, cast on 6 sts, p8—32 sts.
Rows 3–6 Work even in St st.
Row 7 (dec) [K2tog] 16 times—16 sts.
Row 8 Purl.
Row 9 (dec) [K2tog] 8 times—8 sts.
Row 10 (dec) [P2tog] 4 times—4 sts.
Bind off.

FINISHING

HORNS AND TAIL
Fill horns and tail with polyester stuffing. Cut felt circles the same size as horn and tail openings on WS, sew over openings to secure stuffing.

FACE
With yarn needle and A, wrap yarn around the p3tog to gather the snout. Fold hood in place along the sides of face to the cast-on row, sew in place from WS.

FIRE BREATH
Cut red ribbon into several lengths of 1–2"/2.5–5cm. Stack the ribbons, sew them together at one end, and sew this end to WS of snout.

EYES
Arrange beads and eyelashes as foll and glue in place: center the small bead on top of the large bead, place large bead on top of eyelash. Sew or glue eyes to face, centering under each horn.

BACK
Sew scales along the middle knit st on center back of dragon, working from top of hood to tip of tail, in this order: 1 medium, 3 large, 3 medium, 4 small.

WINGS
From RS, wings have 3 purl sections, divided by 2 k sts. With RS facing, C and yarn needle, embroider stem st up center of these 2 sts. Wrap C around back of stem sts on WS, so both sides look good. With RS facing out, sew cast-on edge of wings to each side of upper back. Tack edge of wings to back neck, to hold in place.

BELLY
Sew bobbles to RS of belly.
Pin 4 sts of crotch to center of tail base. Pin each side of belly to sides of dragon, ending at markers. Whip st belly in place from WS. Sew a snap half to both ends of belly cast-on row and to both shoulders at end of the increases, creating armholes.

FEET (make 2)
With larger dpns and D, cast on 10 sts. Join, being careful not to twist sts, and pm for beg of rnd. Knit 4 rnds. Place marker between 5th and 6th sts.
Next (inc) rnd [Kfb, knit to 1 st before marker, kfb, sl marker] twice—14 sts.
Next rnd Rep inc rnd—18 sts.
Next (inc) rnd [Kfb, knit to marker, sl marker] twice—20 sts.
Work even until piece measures 4"/10cm from beg. Bind off.

I-CORD CLAWS
(make 3 for each foot)
With larger dpns and C, cast on 5 sts.
*K5, slide sts to opposite end of needle to work next row from RS, pulling working yarn tightly across back of work. Rep from * until cord measures ¾–1½"/2–4cm from beg, varying the length for each claw.
Next row Ssk, k1, k2tog—3 sts.
Last row SK2P. Fasten off.
Insert cast-on edge of 3 claws into bound-off edge of foot. Sew bound-off edge closed for toe seam. ✳

Curious Cat

*"The Magical Cat Is a Mystery
It Lives Nine Lives So Wild and Free"*

●●●○

MATERIALS
- 1 3½oz/100g skein (each approx 170yd/156m) of Lion Brand *Vanna's Choice* (acrylic) each in #112 raspberry (A) and #100 white (4)
- 1 1½oz/40g skein (each approx 57yd/52m) of Lion Brand *Fun Fur* (polyester) in #300 cotton candy (C) (5)
- One pair each sizes 6 and 8 (4 and 5mm) needles OR SIZE TO OBTAIN GAUGE
- One set (5) each sizes 6 and 8 (4 and 5mm) double-pointed needles (dpns)
- 4 small snaps
- Sewing needle and thread
- Small amount of polyester stuffing
- Stitch markers and stitch holders
- Yarn needle

GAUGE
16 sts and 24 rows to 4"/10cm over St st (knit on RS, purl on WS), using size 8 (5mm) needles and A.
TAKE TIME TO CHECK GAUGE.

STITCH GLOSSARY
CO1 (cast on 1—inc) Wrap yarn around left thumb from back to front. Insert RH needle from front into the loop on thumb. Remove thumb from loop and tighten loop on needle (also called wrap cast-on). 1 stitch has been increased.

NOTES
1) Cat suit is worked in one piece from the neck down.

2) *Fun Fur* can be slippery. Be sure to insert needle completely into stitch to avoid dropping it.

CAT SUIT
With larger needles and B, cast on 56 sts. Knit 1 row on RS.
Beg with a WS row, cont in St st as foll: work 2 rows A, 2 rows C, 2 rows B.

DIVIDE FOR SLEEVES
Row 1 (WS) With A, p10 for right back, bind off 10 sts for right armhole, purl until 16 sts are on needle, bind off 10 sts for left armhole, purl to end—10 left back sts.
Row 2 (RS) With A, k10, cast on 4 sts, k16, cast on 4 sts, k10—44 sts.
Rows 3–6 Work with A.
Row 7 Work with B.
Row 8 (RS) With B, CO1, knit to end, CO1—46 sts.

Cont in St st with C, work even for 4"/10cm, end with a WS row. Cut C. Work 2 rows B, 2 rows A.

DIVIDE FOR LEGS
Place first 23 sts on st holder for right leg.

LEFT LEG
With A and smaller dpn 1, CO1, k7; with dpn 2, k8; with dpn 3, k8, place marker for beg of rnd—24 sts. Knit 1 rnd A. Cont in St st in the rnd (knit every rnd), AT THE SAME TIME, [knit 2 rnds B, knit 2 rnds A] 6 times, knit 2 rnds B. Cut yarn. Join C and cont in St st until leg measures 6"/15cm. Bind off.

RIGHT LEG
Rejoin A and sl 23 sts to 3 smaller dpns as foll: pick up and k 1 st in cast-on st of left leg, k7; with dpn 2, k8; with dpn 3, k8, place marker (pm) for beg of rnd—24 sts. Complete same as left leg.

FINISHING
Sew the back seam, leaving the top 3"/7.5cm open.

TAIL
With smaller dpns and A, cast on 12 sts, divide evenly over 3 needles. Join and pm for beg of rnd. Knit 8 rnds A, 16 rnds C, 8 rnds B. With C only, cont in St st until tail measures 12"/30.5cm from beg. Bind off.
Sew cast-on edge of tail to the back, approx 1½"/4cm below back opening. Sew snaps evenly to back opening.

HOOD

Note Wind off 2 small balls of C to work side edges of hood.

With larger dpns and B, cast on 40 sts, divide evenly over 4 needles. Join and pm for beg of rnd.

Rnds 1–4 (RS) [K2, p2] 10 times.

Rnds 5–8 With A, rep rnds 1–4. Bind off for face opening, remove beg-of-rnd marker and cont to work back and forth in rows as foll:

Row 9 (RS) With A, bind off 12 sts; knit until there are 14 sts on needle, pm, k to end.

Row 10 (WS) Join first ball of C and p6, with B, p to marker, CO1 for center back, slip marker, p to last 6 sts, join 2nd ball of C and p6—29 sts.

SHAPE HOOD

Row 11 (RS) K6 C; with B, knit to marker, CO1, sl marker, k1, CO1, knit to last 6 sts; k6 C—31 sts.

Row 12 P6 C; p19 B; p6 C.

Row 13 K6 C; with A, knit to marker, CO1, sl marker, k1, CO1, knit to last 6 sts; k6 C—33 sts.

Row 14 P6 C; p21 A; p6 C.

Row 15 Rep row 13—35 sts.

Row 16 P6 C; p23 A; p6 C.

Row 17 K6 C; with B, knit to marker, CO1, sl marker, k1, CO1, knit to last 6 sts; k6 C—37 sts.

Row 18 P6 C; p25 B; p6 C.

Row 19 K6 C; with B, CO1, knit to marker, CO1, sl marker, k1, CO1, knit to last 6 sts, CO1; k6 C—41 sts.

Row 20 P6 C; p29 B; p6 C.

Row 21 K6 C; with A, knit to marker, CO1, sl marker, k1, CO1, knit to last 6 sts; k6 C—43 sts.

Row 22 P6 C; p31 A; p6 C.

Row 23 K6 C; with A CO1, knit to marker, CO1, sl marker, k1, CO1, knit to last 6 sts, CO1; k6 C—47 sts.

Row 24 P6 C; p35 A; p6 C.

Row 25 K6 C; with B, knit to marker, CO1, sl marker, k1, CO1, knit to last 6 sts, k6 C—49 sts.

Row 26 P6 C; p37 B; p6 C.

Row 27 K6 C; with B, CO1, knit to marker, sl marker, k1, knit to last 6 sts, CO1; k6 C—51 sts.

Row 28 P6 C; p39 B; p6 C.

Row 29 K6 C; with A, knit to 2 sts before marker, k2tog, sl marker, k1, k2tog, knit to last 6 sts; k6 C—49 sts.

Row 30 P6 C; p37 A; p6 C.

Row 31 Rep row 29—47 sts.

Row 32 P6 C; p35 A; p6 C.

Row 33 K6 C; with B, ssk, knit to 2 sts before marker, k2tog, sl marker, k1, k2tog, knit to last 8 sts, k2tog; k6 C—43 sts.

Row 34 P6 C; p31 B; p6 C.

Row 35 Rep row 33—39 sts.

Row 36 P6 C; p27 B; p6 C. Remove marker.

Row 37 K6 C; with A, [k2tog] 13 times, k1; k6 C—26 sts.

Row 38 P6 C; p14 A; p6 C.

Row 39 K6 C; with A [k2tog] 7 times; k6 C—19 sts.

Row 40 P6 C; p7 A; p6 C.

Row 41 K6 C; with B k1, [k2tog] 3 times; k6 C—16 sts.

Row 42 With C p6, [p2tog] twice, p6—14 sts. With C, bind off.

FINISHING

With RS tog, fold bound-off edge in half at center st, sew tog for top of hood.

EARS

OUTER EAR (MAKE 2)

With A and smaller needles, cast on 8 sts. Work in St st for 4 rows.

Cont in St st and dec 1 st at beg and end of every RS row 3 times—2 sts.

Last row (WS) P2tog. Fasten off.

INNER EAR (MAKE 2)

With B and smaller needles, cast on 6 sts. Work in St st for 4 rows.

Cont in St st and dec 1 st at beg and end of every RS row twice—2 sts.

Last row (WS) P2tog. Fasten off.

FINISHING

With RS of inner ear and outer ear pieces tog, sew along shaped side edges. Turn RS out, fill with stuffing, sew cast-on edges tog for bottom of ear. Using photo as guide, sew ears to top of hood.

MITTS (MAKE 2)

With smaller dpns and C, cast on 16 sts. Divide sts evenly over 4 needles. Join, being careful not to twist sts, and pm for beg of rnd. Knit 3 rnds. Cut C. Join A.

Rnds 1–4 *K2, p2; rep from * around.

Rnds 5–9 Knit.

SHAPE PALM

Rnd 10 [K1, CO1, k6, CO1, k1] twice—20 sts.

Rnd 11 Knit.

Rnd 12 [K1, CO1, k8, CO1, k1] twice—24 sts.

Rnds 13–16 Knit.

Rnd 17 *K2tog; rep from * around—12 sts. Bind off. Turn inside out with RS tog, fold in half and seam. With B and yarn needle, using photo as guide, foll Mitt diagram and work duplicate st on each palm.

PAWS (MAKE 2)

With dpns and A, cast on 10 sts. Divide sts evenly over 3 needles (3 – 4 – 3). Join, being careful not to twist sts, and pm for beg of rnd.

Rnds 1–4 Knit.

Rnd 5 [Kfb, k3, kfb] twice—14 sts.

Rnd 6 Knit.

Rnd 7 [Kfb, k5, kfb] twice—18 sts.

Rnd 8 Knit.

Rnd 9 [Kfb, k8] twice—20 sts.

Work even in St st until piece measures 3"/7.5cm from beg.

Next rnd [K2tog, k6, k2tog] twice—16 sts. Knit 1 rnd. Bind off. Fold in half with RS together and seam. With B and yarn needle, using photo as guide, foll Paw diagram and work duplicate st on palm of each mitt. ✳

PAW DIAGRAM

KEY

ⓥ duplicate stitch in B

Child's Cat Hat & Mitts

"Cute as a Couple of Cats Can Be!"

FINISHED MEASUREMENTS
Instructions are written for one size:
Hood at widest point approx 14½"/37cm
Hood height above neckband 8"/20.5cm

MATERIALS
- 1 3½oz/100g ball (each approx 170yd/156m) of Lion Brand *Vanna's Choice* (acrylic) each in #112 raspberry (A) and #100 white (B)
- 1 1½oz/40g ball (each approx 57yd/52m) of Lion Brand *Fun Fur* (polyester) in #300 cotton candy stripes (C)
- One pair size 8 (5mm) needles OR SIZE TO OBTAIN GAUGE
- Size 8 (5mm) circular needle, 16"/40cm long, for neckband
- One set (5) size 8 (5mm) double-pointed needles (dpns) for mitts
- One set (4) size 6 (4mm) double-pointed needles (dpns) for thumbs
- Yarn needle
- Removable stitch marker
- Small stitch holder

GAUGE
17 sts and 24 rows to 4"/10cm over St st using size 8 (5mm) needles and A or B.
TAKE TIME TO CHECK GAUGE.

STITCH GLOSSARY
CO1 (cast on 1—inc) Wrap yarn around left thumb from back to front. Insert RH needle from front into the loop on thumb. Remove thumb from loop and tighten loop on needle (also called wrap cast-on). 1 stitch has been increased.

NOTE
Wind C into 2 equal balls.

STRIPE PATTERN
Rows 1–6 Work with B.
Rows 7–12 Work with A.
Rep rows 1–12 for stripe pat.

NOTE
Fun Fur can be slippery. Be sure to insert needle completely into stitch to avoid dropping it.

HOOD
NECKBAND
With size 8 (5mm) circular needle and B, cast on 76 sts. Join, being careful not to twist sts, and place marker (pm) for beg of rnd.
Rnds 1–6 With B, *k2, p2; rep from * around. Cut B.
Rnds 7–12 With A, *k2, p2; rep from * around.
Bind off for face opening as foll:
Row 1 (RS) Join first ball C, k12; with B, k14, pm, CO1 for center st, k14; join 2nd ball C, k12; with A [k2tog] twice, *bind off the first A st on RH needle, k2tog; rep from * until last 24 sts have been knit tog and bound off, fasten off last st, and cut A, remove beg-of-rnd marker—53 sts.
Turn, work back and forth in rows of St st (k on RS, p on WS) and stripe pat as foll:
Row 2 (WS) P12 C; with B, p to last 12 sts; p12 C.

SHAPE CENTER
Row 3 (RS) K12 C; with B, knit to marker, CO1, slip marker, k1 (center st), CO1, k to last 12 sts; k12 C—55 sts.
Row 4 P12 C; with B, p to last 12 sts, p12 C.

Cont as established and work rows 5–12 of stripe pat once, AT THE SAME TIME, cont to inc on both sides of center st every RS row 4 more times—63 sts.

SHAPE FRONT
Row 1 (inc) Knit 12 C; with B, kfb, k to last 13 sts, kfb; k12 C—65 sts.
Row 2 P12 C; with B, p to last 12 sts; p12 C.
Row 3–6 Rep rows 1 and 2 twice more—69 sts.
Rows 7–12 Work even in stripe pat as established, ending with stripe pat row 12.

SHAPE TOP
Row 1 K12 C; with B, k to 2 sts before marker, k2tog, sl marker, k1, k2tog, k to last 12 sts; k12 C—67 sts.
Row 2 P12 C; with B, p to last 12 sts, p12 C.
Cont as established in stripe pat and rep dec row every RS row 8 more times, end with a stripe pat row 6—12 C sts, 27 B sts, 12 C sts. Remove marker.
Row 19 K12 C; with A, k1, [k2tog] 6 times, k1, [k2tog] 6 times, k1; k12 C—12 C sts, 15 A sts, 12 C sts.
Rows 20 and 22 P12 C; with B, p to last 12 sts, p12 C.
Row 21 K12 C; with A, k1, [k2tog] 3 times, k1, [k2tog] 3 times, k1; k12 C—12 C sts, 9 A sts, 12 C sts.
Row 23 K12 C; with A, [k2tog] twice, k1, [k2tog] twice; k12 C—12 C sts, 5 A sts, 12 C sts.
Row 24 P12 C; with A, p2tog, p1, p2tog; p12 C—12 C sts, 3 A sts, 12 C sts. Cut A.
Row 25 With C, k12, k3tog, k12.
Bind off rem 25 sts with C.

FINISHING

With RS tog, fold bound-off edge of hood in half at center st, sew tog for top of hood.

EARS

OUTER EAR (MAKE 2)

With straight size 8 (5mm) needles and A, cast on 14 sts. Work in St st for 8 rows. Cont in St st and dec 1 st each side every RS row 6 times—2 sts. **Last row (WS)** P2tog. Fasten off.

INNER EAR (MAKE 2)

With straight size 8 (5mm) needles and B, cast on 12 sts. Work in St st for 6 rows. Cont in St st and dec 1 st each side every RS row 5 times—2 sts. **Last row (WS)** P2tog. Fasten off.

FINISHING

With RS of inner ear and outer ear pieces tog, sew along shaped side edges. Turn piece RS out and sew cast-on edges tog for bottom of ear. Using photo as guide, sew ears to top of hood.

MITT (MAKE 2)

Note Both mitts are worked the same; duplicate st is worked on palm of mitt, which determines left or right.

With straight size 8 (5mm) needles and C, cast on 38 sts. Knit 6 rows. Cut C, leaving a 10"/4cm tail for weaving.

Next row (RS) With A, knit, dividing sts evenly on 4 larger dpns (10–9–10–9). Join to work in the rnd. Place removable marker on first st for beg of rnd.

Rnds 1–5 Knit.

Rnds 6–11 *K1, p1; rep from * around.

DIVIDE FOR THUMB

Rnd 12 Place 10 sts on holder for thumb, k28. **Rnd 13** Cast on 2 sts, k to end—30 sts. Cont in St st (knit every rnd) until piece measures 3"/7.5cm above thumb divide. Bind off.

THUMB

Place 10 thumb sts evenly on 3 smaller dpns (3–4–3), with A, join to work in the rnd, pm for beg of rnd.

Next rnd Pick up and k 1 st in the first cast-on st, k10, pick up and k 1 st in 2nd cast-on st—12 sts. Cut A. With B, knit 4 rnds. Bind off.

FINISHING

With tail of C and tapestry needle, sew side edges closed.

Fold each mitt so that thumb faces front. With B and tapestry needle, use photo as guide for placement, foll paw diagram and work duplicate st on palm of each mitt. ✳

MITT DIAGRAM

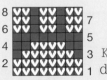

KEY

duplicate stitch in B

8 sts

Knitting Basics

Use these simple step-by-step instructions to share the joy of knitting with the young ones you love. They can use their new skills to make the projects on these pages, all constructed from easy garter stitch squares!

1

Make a slip knot on the right needle, leaving a long tail. Wind the tail end around your left thumb, front to back. Wrap the yarn from the ball around your left index finger and secure both ends in your left palm.

2

Insert the needle upward into the loop of your thumb, as shown.

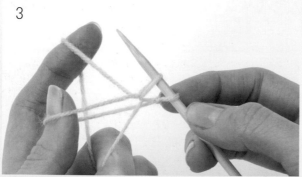

3

Then with the needle, draw the yarn from the ball through the loop to form a stitch on the needle (shown here: the slip knot and the first cast-on stitch).

4

Take your thumb out of the loop and tighten the stitch on the needle, as shown. Repeat Steps 1–4 until the desired number of stitches are cast on.

5

Now you are ready to begin knitting. Hold the needle with the stitches in your left hand and the working yarn in your right hand. Insert the right needle from front to back into the first stitch on the left needle, as shown.

6

Wrap the yarn under and over the right needle in a clockwise motion.

7

With the right needle, catch the yarn just wrapped and pull it through the cast-on stitch, as shown.

8

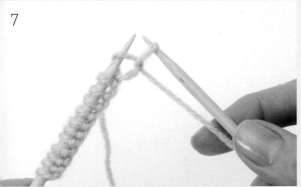

Slip the cast-on stitch off the left needle, leaving the newly formed stitch on the right needle, pull the yarn to tighten the loop a bit. Repeat Steps 5–8 across the row until all of the stitches have been worked.

9

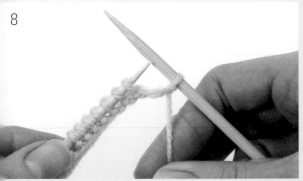

Shown here is the first row of knit stitches.

My First Purse

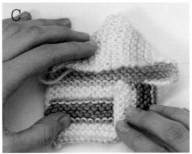

A

To complete the bag, thread tail end of cast-on into a tapestry needle. Fold cast-on edge to the inside, matching corners.

B

Sew the two halves of the cast-on edge together.

C

Fold one corner from the bound-off edge up to meet the side of the sewn corner above.

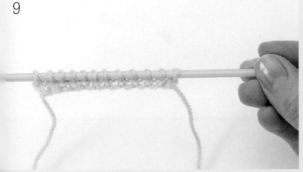

D

Sew the side of the third corner to the side of the adjacent corner. The remaining 4th corner becomes the front flap of the bag.

PURSE
Note Purse can be made to any size. Just cast on fewer or more sts and work in garter st to make a square. See page 114 for materials.

SQUARE (make 1)
With size 6 (4mm) needles, cast on 24 sts. Work in garter st for 4"/10cm. Bind off.

FINISHING
See photos above for folding and seaming. Fold rem corner to outside and sew button to front.

STRAP
With crochet hook, chain approx 7"/18cm. Fasten off. Sew end to top of purse.

113

Pair of Ponchos

Your best girl and her best doll can both be pretty in pink!

●●○○

SIZES
Poncho instructions are for doll's size, with girl's size 4–6 in parentheses. Hat is sized for doll only.

MATERIALS
For Poncho
- 1 (3) 1.4oz/40g skeins (each approx 109yd/100m) of Lion Brand *Jamie Stripes* (acrylic) in #200 pink stripes ③
For Hat or Purse
- 1 ball in #200 pink stripes
- One pair size 6 (4mm) needles OR SIZE TO OBTAIN GAUGE
- Size G/6 (4mm) crochet hook for purse handle
- One small button for purse

GAUGE
24 sts and 42 rows to 4"/10cm over garter st using size 6 (4mm) needles. TAKE TIME TO CHECK GAUGE.

PONCHO
SQUARE (make 4)
With size 6 (4mm) needles, cast on 24 (45) sts. Work in garter st (knit every row) for 4 (7½)"/10 (19)cm. Bind off.

FINISHING
Label 2 squares as A and 2 as B. Lay three squares tog (all in the same direction; that is, cast-on edges at lower edge) with A in the middle and 1 B square either side (see Step 1 diagram). Sew sides of B squares to sides of A square.
Fold top corners of B squares to outside (see dotted line on Step 2 diagram). Sew sides of 2nd A square (see dotted line on Step 3 diagram) to folded sides of B square.

FLOWER
With size 6 (4mm) needles, cast on 42 (72) sts.
Rows 1 and 3 (RS) Knit.
Rows 2 and 4 Purl.
Row 5 *K6, rotate the LH needle counterclockwise 360 degrees, then knit another 6 sts and rotate the LH needle again counterclockwise 360 degrees; rep from * to end.

Row 6 Purl.
Row 7 *K2tog; rep from * to end—21 (36) sts.
Row 8 *P2tog; rep from *, end p1 (p2tog)—11 (18) sts.
Row 9 *K2tog; rep from *, end k1 (k2tog)—6 (9) sts.
Cut yarn and thread through rem sts. Pull tightly.
Twist to form a rose shape.
Sew to front of poncho.

HAT
SQUARE (make 2)
With size 6 (4mm) needles, cast on 36 sts. Work in garter st (knit every row) for 6"/15.5cm. Bind off.

FINISHING
Sew three sides of squares tog, leaving 4th side open.

FLOWER
With size 6 (4mm) needles, cast on 42 sts. Work same as for poncho.

CORKSCREW TASSELS (make 4)
With size 6 (4mm) needles, cast on 20 sts.
Row 1 Knit in front, back, and front of each st—60 sts. Bind off purlwise. Use fingers to twist each tassel into a corkscrew. Attach 2 tassels to each corner at top of hat.
Fold brim of hat to RS and sew flower at center (see photo).

Poncho–Step 1

Sew sides of B squares to sides of A squares

Poncho–Step 2
neck opening

Fold B squares (along dotted line)

Poncho–Step 3

Sew sides of 2nd A square (along dotted line) to sides of B squares

Templates

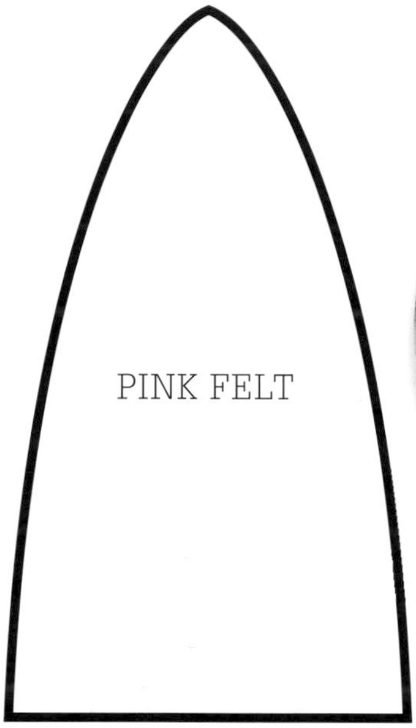

PINK FELT

Noble Unicorn's Ear
(page 32)

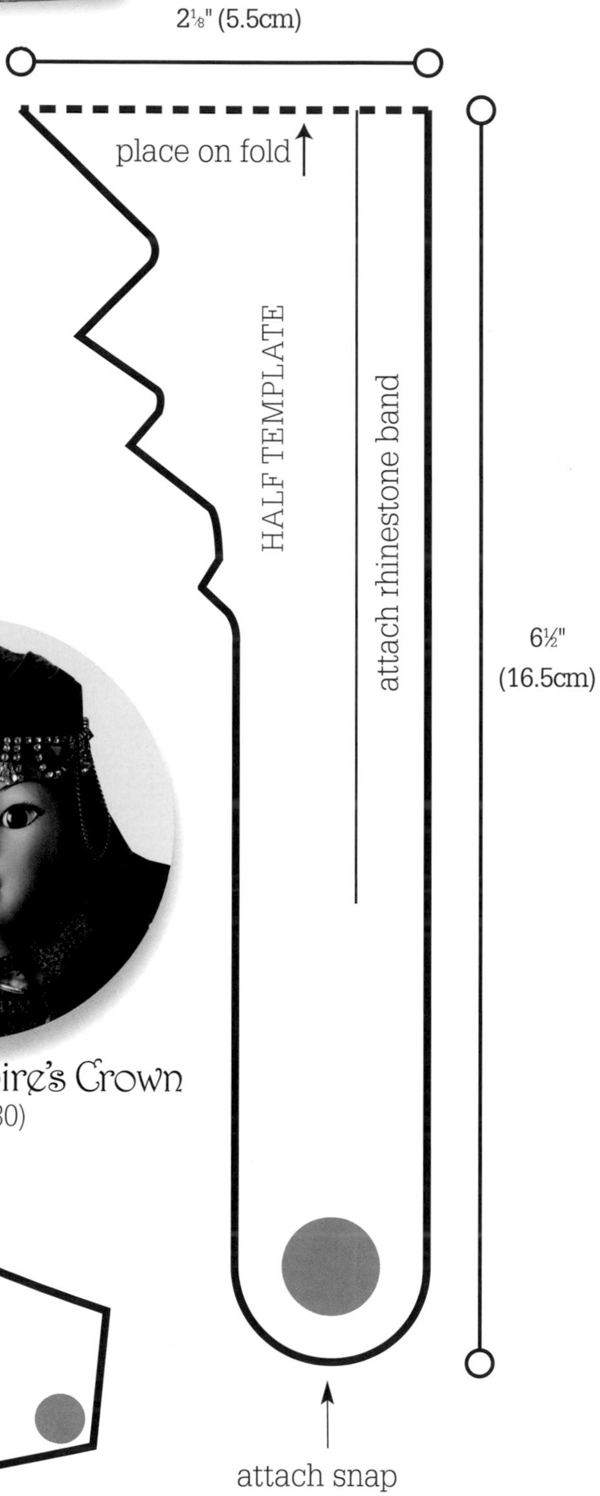

Magical Dragon's Cuff
(page 102)

Madame Vampire's Crown
(page 80)

2⅛" (5.5cm)

place on fold ↑

HALF TEMPLATE

attach rhinestone band

6½"
(16.5cm)

attach snap

LEATHER-LIKE FABRIC

attach snap

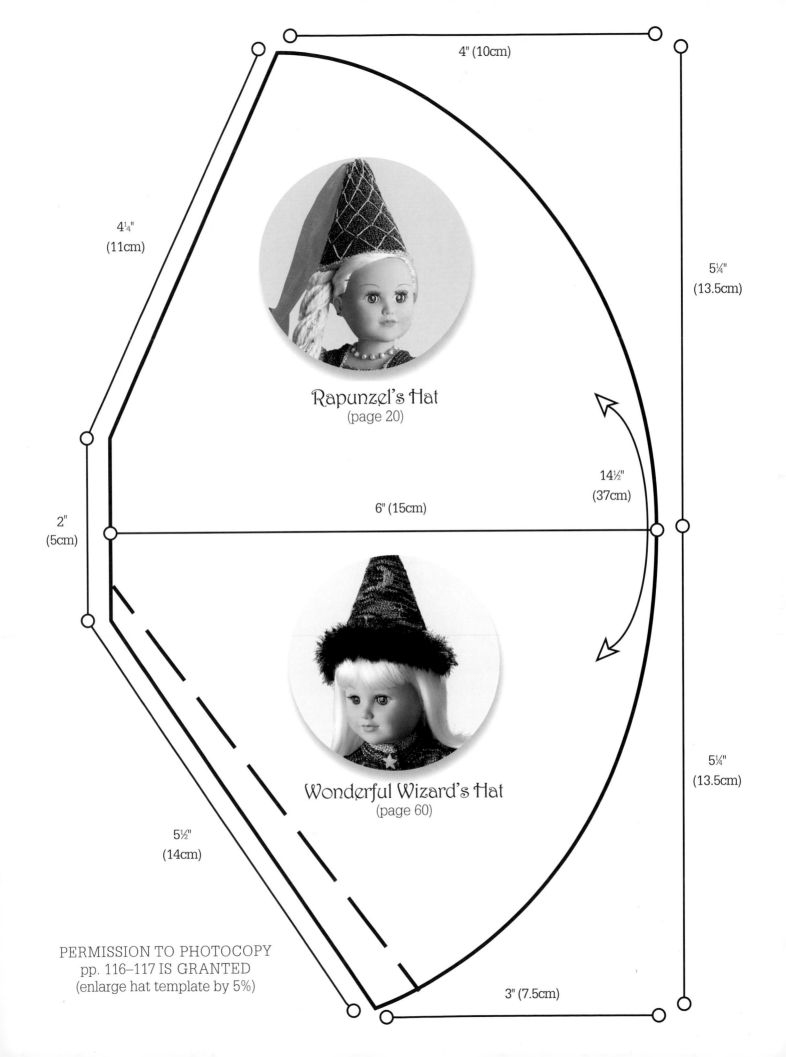

4" (10cm)

4¼" (11cm)

5¼" (13.5cm)

Rapunzel's Hat
(page 20)

2" (5cm)

6" (15cm)

14½" (37cm)

Wonderful Wizard's Hat
(page 60)

5½" (14cm)

5¼" (13.5cm)

3" (7.5cm)

Enchanted Info

Abbreviations

approx	approximately
beg	begin(ning)
CC	contrasting color
ch	chain
cm	centimeter(s)
cn	cable needle
cont	continu(e)(ing)
dec	decreas(e)(ing)
dpn(s)	double-pointed needle(s)
foll	follow(s)(ing)
g	gram(s)
inc	increas(e)(ing)
k	knit
kfb	knit into the front and back of a stitch—one stitch increased
k2tog	knit 2 stitches together—one stitch decreased
LH	left-hand
lp(s)	loop(s)
m	meter(s)
mm	millimeter(s)
MC	main color
M1 or M1L	make one or make one left (see glossary)
M1 p-st	make one purl stitch (see glossary)
M1R	make one right (see glossary)
oz	ounce(s)
p	purl
pfb	purl into front and back of a stitch—one stitch increased
pat(s)	pattern(s)
pm	place marker
psso	pass slip stitch(es) over
p2tog	purl two stitches together—one stitch has been decreased

Standard Yarn Weight System

Categories of yarn, gauge ranges, and recommended needle and hook sizes

Yarn Weight Symbol & Category	0 Lace	1 Super Fine	2 Fine	3 Light	4 Medium	5 Bulky	6 Super Bulky	7 Jumbo
Type of Yarns in Category	Fingering 10-count crochet thread	Sock, Fingering, Baby	Sport, Baby	DK, Light Worsted	Worsted, Afghan, Aran	Chunky, Craft, Rug	Super Bulky, Roving	Jumbo, Roving
Knit Gauge Range* in Stockinette Stitch to 4 inches	33–40** sts	27–32 sts	23–26 sts	21–24 sts	16–20 sts	12–15 sts	7–11 sts	6 sts and fewer
Recommended Needle in Metric Size Range	1.5–2.25 mm	2.25—3.25	3.25—3.75 mm	3.75—4.5 mm	4.5—5.5 mm	5.5—8 mm	8—12.75 mm	12.75 mm and larger
Recommended Needle U.S. Size Range	000–1	1 to 3	3 to 5	5 to 7	7 to 9	9 to 11	11 to 17	17 and larger
Crochet Gauge* Ranges in Single Crochet to 4 inch	32–42 double crochets**	21–32 sts	16–20 sts	12–17 sts	11–14 sts	8–11 sts	6–9 sts	5 sts and fewer
Recommended Hook in Metric Size Range	Steel*** 1.6–1.4 mm	2.25—3.5 mm	3.5—4.5 mm	4.5—5.5 mm	5.5—6.5 mm	6.5—9 mm	9—16 mm	16 mm and larger
Recommended Hook U.S. Size Range	Steel*** 6, 7, 8 Regular hook B-1	B–1 to E–4	E–4 to 7	7 to I–9	I–9 to K–10 1/2	K–10 1/2 to M–13	M–13 to Q	Q and larger

* GUIDELINES ONLY: The above reflect the most commonly used gauges and needle or hook sizes for specific yarn categories.

** Lace weight yarns are usually knitted or crocheted on larger needles and hooks to create lacy, openwork patterns. Accordingly, a gauge range is difficult to determine. Always follow the gauge stated in your pattern.

*** Steel crochet hooks are sized differently from regular hooks—the higher the number, the smaller the hook, which is the reverse of regular hook sizing

This Standards & Guidelines booklet and downloadable symbol artwork are available at: **YarnStandards.com**

rem	remain(s)(ing)	**SK2P**	slip 1, knit 2 together, pass slip stitch over the k2tog—two stitches decreased
rep	repeat		
RH	right-hand		
RS	right side(s)		
rnd(s)	round(s)	**S2KP**	slip 2 stitches together, knit 1, pass 2 slip stitches over knit 1
SKP	slip 1, knit 1, pass slip stitch over—one stitch decreased		

Enchanted Info

Abbreviations (cont.)

sc	single crochet
sl	slip
sl st	slip stitch
spp	slip, purl, pass sl st over
ssk (ssp)	slip 2 sts knitwise one at a time, insert LH needle through fronts of sts and knit (purl) together
sssk	slip 3 sts one at a time knitwise, insert LH needle through fronts of sts and knit together
st(s)	stitch(es)
St st	stockinette stitch
tbl	through back loop(s)
tog	together
WS	wrong side(s)
wyib	with yarn in back
wyif	with yarn in front
yd(s)	yd(s)
yo	yarn over needle
*****	repeat directions following * as indicated

Gauge

Make a test swatch at least 4"/10cm square. If the number of stitches and rows does not correspond to the gauge given, you must change the needle size. An easy rule to follow is: To get fewer stitches to the inch/cm, use a larger needle; to get more stitches to the inch/cm, use a smaller needle. Continue to try different needle sizes until you get the same number of stitches in the gauge.

Glossary

bind off Used to finish an edge or segment. Lift the first stitch over the second, the second over the third, etc. (U.K.: cast off)

bind off in rib or pat Work in rib or pat as you bind off. (Knit the knit stitches, purl the purl stitches.)

cast on Place a foundation row of stitches upon the needle in order to begin knitting.

decrease Reduce the stitches in a row (for example, knit two together).

increase Add stitches in a row (for example, knit in front and back of stitch).

knitwise Insert the needle into the stitch as if you were going to knit it.

make one or make one left Insert left-hand needle from front to back under the strand between last st worked and next st on left-hand needle. Knit into the back loop to twist the stitch.

make one p-st Insert needle from front to back under the strand between the last stitch worked and the next stitch on the left-hand needle. Purl into the back loop to twist the stitch.

make one right Insert left-hand needle from back to front under the strand between the last stitch worked and the next stitch on left-hand needle. Knit into the front loop to twist the stitch.

no stitch On some charts, "no stitch" is indicated with shaded spaces where stitches have been decreased or not yet made. In such cases, work the stitches of the chart, skipping over the "no stitch" spaces.

place marker Place or attach a loop of contrast yarn or purchased stitch marker as indicated.

pick up and knit (purl) Knit (or purl) into the loops along an edge.

purlwise Insert the needle into the stitch as if you were going to purl it.

selvage stitch Edge stitch that helps make seaming easier.

slip, slip, knit Slip next two stitches knitwise, one at a time, to right-hand needle. Insert tip of left-hand needle into fronts of these stitches, from left to right. Knit them together. One stitch has been decreased.

slip, slip, slip, knit Slip next three stitches knitwise, one at a time, to right-hand needle. Insert tip of left-hand needle into fronts of these stitches, from left to right. Knit them together. Two stitches have been decreased.

slip stitch An unworked stitch made by passing a stitch from the left-hand to the right-hand needle as if to purl.

work even Continue in pattern without increasing or decreasing. (U.K.: work straight)

yarn over Make a new stitch by wrapping the yarn over the right-hand needle. (U.K.: yfwd, yon, yrn).

Skill Levels

Beginner
Ideal first project.

Intermediate
For knitters with some experience. More intricate stitches, shaping, and finishing.

Easy
Basic stitches, minimal shaping, and simple finishing.

Experienced
For knitters able to work patterns with complicated shaping and finishing

Enchanted Info

Basic Stitches

Garter Stitch
Knit every row.

Circular Knitting
Knit one round, then purl one round.

Stockinette Stitch
Knit right-side rows and purl wrong-side rows.

Circular Knitting
Knit every round.

Reverse Stockinette Stitch
Purl right-side rows and knit wrong-side rows.

Circular Knitting
Purl every round.

Seed Stitch
Row 1 (RS) *Knit 1, purl 1, repeat from * to end.
Row 2 (RS) Knit the purl stitches and purl the knit stitches.
Rep row 2 for seed stitch.

Knitting Needle Sizes

U.S.	Metric
0	2mm
1	2.25mm
2	2.75mm
3	3.25mm
4	3.5mm
5	3.75mm
6	4mm
7	4.5mm
8	5mm
9	5.5mm
10	6mm
10½	6.5mm
11	8mm
13	9mm
15	10mm
17	12.75mm
19	15mm
35	19mm

Knitting with Double-Pointed Needles (using 4 needles)

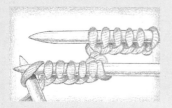 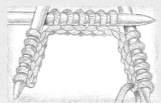 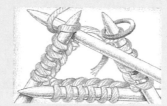

1. Cast on one-third the required number of stitches on the first needle, plus one. Slip this extra stitch to the next needle as shown. Continue in this way, casting on the remaining stitches on the last needle.

2. Arrange the needles as shown, with the cast-on edge facing the center of the triangle (or square).

3. Place a stitch marker after the last cast-on stitch. With the fee needle, knit the first cast-on stitch, pulling the yarn tightly. Continue knitting in rounds, slipping the marker before beginning each round.

Crochet Hook Sizes

U.S.	Metric
B/1	2mm
C/2	2.75mm
D/3	3.25mm
E/4	3.5mm
F/5	3.75mm
G/6	4mm
7	4.5mm
H/8	5mm
I/9	5.5mm
J/10	6mm
K/10½	6.5mm
L/11	8mm
M/13	9mm
N/15	10mm

Embroidery

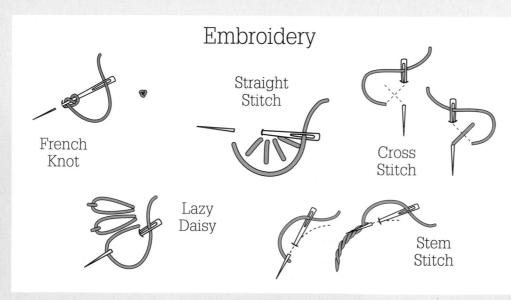

French Knot

Straight Stitch

Cross Stitch

Lazy Daisy

Stem Stitch

Enchanted Info

Duplicate Stitch

Duplicate stitch covers a knit stitch. Bring the needle up below the stitch to be worked. Insert the needle under both loops one row above and pull it through. Insert it back into the stitch below and through the center of the next stitch in one motion, as shown.

Crochet Chain Stitch

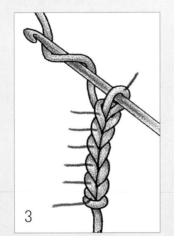

1. Draw the yarn through the loop on the hook by catching it with the hook and pulling it toward you.

2. One chain stitch is complete. Lightly tug on the yarn to tighten the loop if it is very loose, or wiggle the hook to loosen the loop if it is very tight.

3. Repeat steps 1 and 2 to make as many chain stitches as required for your pattern.

Single Crochet

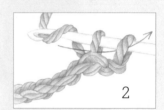

1. Insert hook through top two loops of a stitch. Pass yarn over hook and draw up a loop—two loops on hook.

2. Pass yarn over hook and draw through both loops on hook.

3. Continue in the same way, inserting hook into each stitch.

Provisional Cast-On

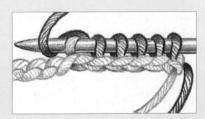

With scrap yarn, make a crochet chain a few stitches longer than the number of stitches to be cast on. With main yarn, pick up one stitch in the back loop of each chain. To knit from the cast-on edge, carefully unpick the chain, placing the live stitches one by one on a needle.

Enchanted Info

How to Sew a Crinoline

Note: Doll crinoline can also be purchased online or in stores that sell doll clothing.

MATERIALS
- 1yd/1m of tulle
- Sewing needle and thread
- 11"/28cm of fabric binding OR 11"/28cm of ¾"/20mm ribbon for waist
- 1 small snap

CRINOLINE
Fold netting in half and cut at the fold.

Cut both layers to a length of 9"/23cm, or desired length to fit doll costume.

At waist, using sewing machine or by hand, work 2 rows of running stitch, one at ⅛"/3mm and one at ½"/12mm from top edge, through all layers.

Pull threads gently and gather to fit doll's waist, leaving ¼"/6mm of fabric free at each end. Secure threads.

Fold binding or ribbon in half over the gathers and sew to secure the gathers in place.

Sew snap to each end of gathered fabric/binding to close waistband. (Note: crinoline back seam does not need to be sewn.)

Red Riding Hood (page 42)

Guardian Angel (page 88)

Golden Princess (page 64)

Resources

NOTE: Most of the embellishments (beads, ribbon, etc.) used in the designs can be purchased at any craft store.

BERGÈRE DE FRANCE
Bergeredefrance.com

BERROCO, INC.
Berroco.com

BE SWEET
Besweetproducts.com

CRYSTAL PALACE YARNS
Straw.com

FILATURA DI CROSA
Tahkistacycharles.com

LION BRAND YARN CO.
Lionbrand.com

PATONS
Yarnspirations.com/patons

PLYMOUTH YARN CO.
Plymouthyarn.com

PREMIER YARNS
Premieryarns.com

ROWAN
Knitrowan.com

SCHULANA
Skacelknitting.com

TAHKI•STACY CHARLES, INC.
Tahkistacycharles.com

*Curious Cat
(page 106)*

Acknowledgments

Many thanks to these enchanting, enchanted people:

Royalty: Trisha Malcolm and Art Joinnides, for their encouraging and enthusiastic support.

Wizard: Joe Vior, the amazing creative director, tireless worker, and visionary who brought to this book true enchantment and a look unlike any other book of doll knits. His enthusiasm and dedication to artistic excellence, from the day he took on the project, through the entire process, were awe-inspiring.

Magician: Jack Deutsch, whose exquisite photography and lighting gave vibrant life to these dolls and made my designs look so spectacular. And thanks to his hardworking happy-go-lucky elves Steve Regenato and Keith Greenbaum.

Good Witches: Managing editor Laura Cooke and senior editor Lisa Silverman, who combined all the ingredients in their witches' brew of creativity to turn out a lovely, bewitching book.

Sorcerers: Technical editors Carla Scott, Lori Steinberg, Lisa Buccellato, and Loretta Dachman, who waved their magic wands and got the tough stuff done.

Fairy Godmothers: My intrepid knitters, whom I could not do without, who beautifully and tirelessly transformed many of my designs into reality and met the tight deadlines—Jo Brandon, Emily Brenner, Eileen Curry, Nancy Henderson, and Dianne Weitzul.

Sorcerer's Apprentice: Heris Stenzel, who expertly typed and kept track of all the instructions.

Big Bad Wolf: Ken Epstein, for his creative costume consultation.

Pixie: Diane Lamphron, art director whose lovely suggestions spiced things up.

Princesses: My devoted friends who spurred me on—Morgan Cole, Angie DeFazio, Ann Denton, Sui Der, Christine Farrow, Leigh Merrifield, Phyllis Ross, Susan Sinclair, Mary Spagnuolo, Dana Quinones, and Dana Vessa.

My Knight in Shining Armor: Howard "Lancelot" Epstein, who put up with my long working hours, offered opinions and advice, and endured being surrounded by 25 dolls for over a month, who began to stare at him. He also wrote the descriptive and humorous rhyming couplets that go with each doll.

Other Doll Books by Nicky Epstein

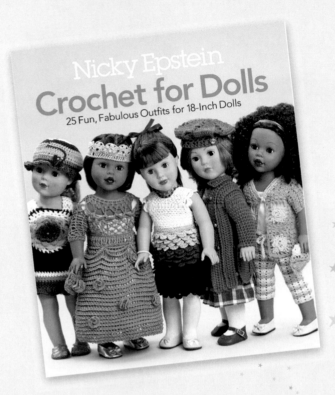

Index

"Come with us on an enchanted journey!"